Our Inner World of Rage

Our Inner World of Rage

Understanding and Transforming the Power of Anger

Lucy Freeman

CONTINUUM • NEW YORK

1990

The Continuum Publishing Company
370 Lexington Avenue
New York, NY 10017

Printed in the United States of America

Library of Congress Cataloging-in-Publication Data

Freeman, Lucy.
Our inner world of rage : understanding and transforming the power
of anger / Lucy Freeman.
p.   cm.
ISBN 0-8264-0471-5
1. Anger. I. Title.
BF575.A5F73   1990
152.4′7—dc20   89-29182
                                                        CIP

Contents

Acknowledgments

My deepest thanks go to Michael Leach, publisher of Continuum, Evander Lomke, managing editor, and Bruce Cassiday, who edited the final manuscript, for their invaluable help all along the way.

1 🎯 The Rage in Our Hearts

During a dinner dance held at a luxurious mansion in New York City a prominent Wall Street broker dances with a pretty blonde, to whom he has just been introduced. His wife, glass of scotch in hand, looks on from the sidelines. She feels a sudden rage, knows he has had several scotches and will flirt with the stranger.

After the music ends and he returns to her side, she says not a word. But later after they return home she attacks with words. She charges, "I saw you flirting with that blonde. Did you make a date to see her again?"

He shakes his head, looks at her sadly, says, "One dance doesn't make me a Casanova. I'll probably never see her again. When will you accept it's you I love? Even though I like to dance with other women."

She hated herself for being so jealous but could not control her feelings. Rage seems natural when someone we love flirts with someone we deem a rival. We either learn to control it or, like this woman, express it, hoping our marital partner will understand.

A mother sees her nine-year-old son walk into their Rye, New York, home, his shoes muddy, his shirt dirty, holding a baseball bat. He tracks the mud across the living-room rug, an heirloom for three generations. She screams, "How many times do I have to tell you to take off your dirty shoes before you walk into this room after a game?"

He winces, says, "Sorry, I forgot."

"You enjoy making me mad!" she goes on. "This rug is—"

"I know, I know," he says. "I'll remember next time."

She sighs, rage retreating, hopes next time he will be thoughtful enough to remember.

Two men who have known each other twenty years, since college, meet occasionally for lunch. One is an executive in an advertising agency, the other is a writer, fairly successful with murder mysteries.

The advertising executive arrives promptly at noon at the Pierre Hotel on Fifth Avenue in Manhattan where they have arranged to meet. He waits in a chair in the small lobby as ten minutes, then fifteen pass, and his rage mounts. He thinks, **Why** is this selfish man always late? Can't he consider anyone else?

Five minutes later the writer bursts through the door, out of breath, apologizes, "I'm so sorry. Got caught on the phone with an editor. My bread and butter, you know."

The advertising executive calms down as he always does, mutters, "I know you couldn't help it," and they walk into the dining room to eat and to compare notes on their lives in the past few months.

The next morning the advertising executive describes his rage during his hour on the psychoanalytic couch. He asks plaintively, "Was I wrong in being so angry? He's always so damned late!"

The analyst replies, "You're entitled to be angry when someone arrives late. It is inconsiderate. But you also want his friendship so you bury your rage. Maybe sometime you'll ask him gently why he is always late. Or maybe you'll just accept his idiosyncracies and not always be on time yourself."

Most of us, being human and trying to act civilized, carry a certain amount of energy within us that, at a second's notice, may be mobilized to express the feeling of rage. This book will describe the anger that is natural to all of us when we feel diminished by another person, hurt by some unjustified personal remark or an act of cruelty. But if we can accept that to diminish our rage eases our emotional state, that angry outbursts may keep us from loving relationships and from feeling a sense of self-esteem, we are likely to feel much happier.

What do we mean when we say we feel enraged? Is rage similar to anger, fury, wrath? Or are there differences among the words we use to express the feeling of rage?

Rage is defined in *Webster's New World Dictionary* as "violent outbursts of anger in which self-control is lost." *Anger* is described as "a feeling that may result from injury, mistreatings, opposition; usually shows a desire to hit out at something else; wrath; indignation; rage; ire." Here rage is defined as similar to anger.

On the other hand the definition of the word *fury* "implies an overwhelming rage of a frenzied kind that borders on madness." Whereas the word *wrath* connotes "deep indignation expressing itself in a desire to punish or get revenge; intense anger; rage; fury." And the word *ire* is "chiefly a literary word, suggests a show of great anger in acts, words, looks, etc."

It would appear that rage, anger, fury, ire and wrath are fairly interchangeable. Anger can rise to the heights of fury and rage, while fury, rage, ire and wrath all hold anger within, by definition. Thus we might think of rage as an amalgam of powerful emotions in which anger may be a central force.

"He that is slow to anger is better than the mighty," according to Proverbs 16:32; which advocates self-control over action. Aristotle acknowledged the value of normal, justified anger: "Those who do not show anger at things that ought to arouse anger are regarded as fools; so too if they do not show anger in the right way, the right time or at the right person."

He defined anger as "an impulse attended with pain to avenge an undeserved slight openly manifested toward ourselves or friends," a "legitimate emotion," one that may at times save our lives. He added, "Certain passions serve as armament," protection of the vulnerable self. He saw the only restrictions on anger to be "at the right time, place and right degree and duration."

Seneca defined anger as the desire for avenging injury. He believed it cost mankind "more than any plague"; that "man is born for mutual help, anger for mutual destruction."

The word "rage" appeared in William Congreve's play, *The Mourning Bride,* written in 1697, holding the famous lines, "Heaven has no rage like love to hatred turned, / Nor hell a fury like a woman scorned." Here rage and fury appear as one and the same.

Psychoanalysts think of rage as an instinct we all possess that may be used either to save our life or slowly destroy it if we are not aware when it is intense—the cause of an addiction like drugs or alcoholism. We need the feeling of rage to survive, for instance, if we must act promptly to race out of the way of a car whose driver has lost control. Or to escape someone who wishes to harm us in any way.

Anger and fear are the two basic emotions we use in times of stress and emergency. Our first reaction is fear if someone threatens our life. This is followed by the angry feelings that enable us to act—run away, jump aside or strike back if someone attacks us with weapons or even words, civilization's soft sword.

The key to our understanding of the rage that lies within, often dormant, is to become aware of the great difference between our realistic rage and our unrealistic rage. Realistic rage is a justified rage that emerges naturally each time we feel threatened by something that is part of reality.

Unrealistic rage, on the other hand, arises from memories and fantasies of wishes for revenge that we carry from childhood. These thwarted wishes, based on our feelings, lie in all of us to some degree. No one escapes the early fantasies concocted to protect our as yet vulnerable psyche from what we construe as dangers.

The amount of happiness in our later life may depend on how much we are aware of the difference between the real rage and the unreal rage that has been stored in the unconscious part of our mind over the years. If we have felt much unreal rage, we may hate ourselves or others more than we love ourselves or others. We may wish to commit murder or actually kill, out of a fiery need for revenge that demands the death of someone we believe has emotionally harmed us without cause.

Or we may turn the wrath on ourselves rather than the villain who has wounded us. We may slowly consume ourselves physically and/or emotionally with anger, afraid to strike out at the one who originally hurt us, made us feel like a nobody, as though we had no body or mind.

If as an adult we can become aware of the reasons for our unreal rage, accept the rage that is based on reality, we find we feel far more at ease within ourselves and with those we love. We accept also the right to direct rage at those who actually hurt us, addressing them in a quiet but firm, justified way rather than a furious, threatening one. When we know we are in the right and deserve to be angry at someone who has maligned us, rage is no longer a compulsion but has become a "right."

The wish to kill has been strong throughout so-called civilization. If rage were not so prevalent among mankind, there would have been world peace long ago. Projection of our anger on another—claiming he is the one out to destroy us—is as old as primitive man.

Projection is one of our mind's defensive, automatic ways of ridding ourselves of blame, at least temporarily. In this way we deny our own rage. As hatred mounts, we point our fingers at someone else, accuse them, "*You* are full of hate."

One woman, who was studying law, at first accepted a close friend's charges that she was "full of hate, never spoke honestly, tried to cover up her deep feelings." This woman was going to a therapist, whereas her friend, who verbally assaulted her, refused to seek help though she confessed she felt miserable most of the time.

The woman in analysis asked her analyst what to do about her hurt feelings. He said, "Don't you understand that your friend is accusing you of all the things she does but cannot face in herself? This is a common way people try to get rid of their own anger. It works for the moment, then the hateful feelings return, as strong as ever. Perhaps stronger, since part of her now feels new guilt, knowing she has unfairly blamed you."

Freud said, "What is alone of value in mental life is . . . the feelings. . . . Ideas are repressed only because they are associated with the release of feelings which the person believes he should not have." Should not have because they are founded not on reality but on his own destructive fantasies.

Sometimes we deny we are angry, wishing to be thought a pleasant, peaceful person. But if in any way we feel hurt or betrayed, in the unconscious part of our mind we automatically will feel homicidal and want to strike back, to go in for the kill. To our unconscious, the mere wish makes the deed come true as we seek to get even for being hated, exploited, manipulated, frustrated, humiliated.

The rage within us is somehow connected to the rage that causes men to want to destroy the world, blow up other nations as well as seeking to blow up their own. What causes this wholesale rage and is there anything we can do to control such wide-scale fury?

Freud did not think so. In his famous *The Future of an Illusion*—the illusion being to bring peace to the world—he spoke of the tendency in so-called civilized man to wage war, as "uncivilized" man had always done in the past.

Freud began by saying, "There are only a few people who can survey human activity in its full compass. Most people have been obliged to restrict themselves to a single, or a few, fields of it. But the less a man knows about the past and the present, the more insecure must prove to be his judgment of the future."

There is the further difficulty in a judgment of this kind, he added, that "the subjective expectations of the individual play a part which it is difficult to assess; and these turn out to be dependent on purely personal factors in his own experience, on the greater or lesser optimism of his attitude to life, as it has been dictated for him by his temperament or by his success or failure."

Freud then described "every individual" as "virtually an enemy of civilization, though civilization is supposed to be an object of universal human interest." Most men, he said, feel "as a heavy burden" the sacrifices civilization expects of them in order to make a communal life possible. Regulations, institutions and commands are directed to the task not only at bringing about a certain distribution of wealth but at maintaining that distribution—"indeed, they have to protect everything that contributes to the conquest of nature and the production of wealth against men's hostile impulses."

He added that we receive the impression that civilization is something imposed "on a resisting majority by a minority which understood how to obtain possession of the means to power and coercion. One would think that a re-ordering of human relations should be possible, which would remove the sources of dissatisfaction with civilization by renouncing coercion and the suppression of the instincts, so that, undisturbed by internal discord, men might devote themselves to the acquisition of wealth and its enjoyment."

But, he concludes, it is questionable if such a state of affairs can be realized, for "it seems rather that every civilization must be built up on coercion and renunciation of instinct. One has, I think, to reckon with the fact that there are present in all men destructive, and therefore anti-social and anti-cultural trends and that in a great number of people these are strong enough to determine their behavior in human society."

He described the "masses" as "lazy and unintelligent; they have no love for instinctual renunciation, and they are not to be convinced by argument of its inevitability." These large numbers of persons "support one another in giving free rein to their indiscipline."

He expressed the hope that new generations, "who have been brought up in kindness and taught to have a high opinion of reason, and who have experienced the benefits of civilization at an early age, will have a different attitude. They will feel it as a possession of their very own and will be ready for its sake to make the sacrifices as regards work and instinctual satisfaction that are necessary for its preservation."

If no culture has so far produced human masses of such quality, this is because no culture has yet devised regulations that will influence men in this way, "and in particular from childhood onwards," he said.

Freud was referring to the "narcissism" of the child who believes the world is his. That no wish of his should be denied. That his comfort comes above all else. That he does not have to work to be fed, bathed, clothed, loved.

It is undoubtedly no coincidence that when a nation feels it endangers the lives of its inhabitants through its own wish to wage war, it is more likely to seek peace with other nations.

The internationally known psychohistorian, Lloyd DeMause, founder of the International Psychohistorical Association, points out that leaders of nations carry out the hostile, unconscious and at times conscious wishes of the populace when war on other nations is declared. In their choice of leaders, the people reveal the rage in their own hearts.

DeMause, editor of the *Journal of Psychohistory*, describes psychohistory as "founded on the findings of Freud—a science in a hurry, racing against man's spiralling ability to destroy himself." He points out that delay in improving the quality of the ozone layer, which protects us from the sun's destructive rays, shows an unconscious suicidal wish.

On a more cheerful note, one way our rage may be expressed indirectly, benefiting ourselves and others, is through humor. In jokes, wit, irony, caricature, sarcasm, we rid ourselves of some of our repressed rage in laughter.

Poets have sensed this way of releasing anger. Goethe wrote of one of his contemporaries, "Where he cracks a joke, there lies a concealed problem."

Laughter becomes important as shown by the pleasure we get in listening to or telling a joke. We speak of being "in a good humor" when we feel cheerful—it is certainly more pleasurable to laugh than to cry and others like us better when we laugh, rather than complain or look depressed.

"Laugh and the world laughs with you; cry and you cry alone." As we laugh, we feel the master of ourselves for the moment. We have somehow managed, instead of murdering someone we hate, at least to ridicule him.

Humor gives us momentary pleasure by removing an inhibition. The pleasure results from lowering psychic tension as our conscience relaxes its vigilance. So much of our daily life is spent in what often seems a losing struggle for freedom: freedom from parental tyranny, from our own self-imposed tyrannies, from the controls of society. As we laugh, we feel free of the rage within.

We are not allowed to express our anger in action but we may belittle, scorn and try to defeat our enemies through laughter and putdowns at their expense. We may try to make those we despise look ridiculous through caricature, satire, sarcasm. As a few comedians did with President Reagan during his administration, for even those at the top may be included in our wrath.

We may even verbally attack little children as W. C. Fields did in his films. We can even attack that most sacred of subjects—mother love. In the play *Fade Out—Fade In*, Carol Burnett brought down the house when, as an aspiring movie star who finally achieves success, she says,

"I owe it all to my mother and her complete lack of faith in me. If she hadn't kept discouraging me over the years, I wouldn't be where I am today."

One woman, who became a highly paid business executive in Manhattan, told her psychoanalyst proudly, "I was able to rise to the top in the work I wanted to do because ever since I was a little girl I kept telling myself I would never be just a slavey housewife like my mother. Never, never, never!"

Through the use of humor, the downtrodden child within us may feel superior to overbearing parents unmasked for the moment as human, rather than godlike, or even, in our fantasy, less than human. Much humor arises at the expense of those in authority suddenly relegated to an inferior position so we may temporarily feel superior.

We make fun of authority in many ways, including our newspaper headlines. The Consolidated Edison Company caused New Yorkers great inconvenience when its workers jammed traffic for days as they ripped up the streets (repairing old equipment). The company's slogan, intended to appease irritated New Yorkers, was "Dig we must! For a Greater New York."

When one newspaper reported that the taxpayers had been denied a look into the books of Consolidated Edison as it asked a rise in its gas and electricity rates, *The Daily News* headlined this, "Dig we mustn't!"

We first enjoy the comic as alleviation of our rage as children, when it appears in concrete situations such as acts, behavior and appearance, like the clown in the circus. Then as we mature we laugh at funny stories and verbal jokes, followed by wit, the highest and most subtle form of humor, according to Dr. Martin Grotjahn in *Beyond Laughter*. Wit appeals to our intellect, as well as giving release to our repressions as, for the moment, guilt and rage fly out the window.

A master at the witty remark, the late Ben Hecht created one of the most humorous last lines ever to end a play in *The Front Page*, which he wrote with Charles MacArthur. The hard-boiled city editor has supposedly just forgiven his star reporter, Hildy Johnson, for the unforgivable sin of wanting to marry and leave the Chicago newspaper to live in New York, the home of his fiancée.

The city editor, in a moment of apparent contrition, shakes hands with his reporter, apologizes for having stood in his way, congratulates him and presents as a wedding gift his own, long-cherished, expensive watch. Then, no sooner has the reporter left the city room than the editor picks up the phone and asks to be connected to the police department.

As the curtain falls, he is instructing the police to arrest the reporter as he boards the train to New York, explaining, "The son-of-a-bitch stole my watch!"

Nonsense of the Alice-in-Wonderland variety appeals to both adults and children as the absurd brings laughter. A man who told the following "shaggy-dog" story noticed that all persons ranging in age from five to fifty roared at his punch line.

A guest was served fish at a dinner, followed by a silver bowl laden with tartar sauce. But instead of putting the sauce on the fish, he plunged his hands into the tartar sauce, then ran his hands through his hair.

His shocked neighbor asked, "Do you realize what you are doing with that tartar sauce?"

"Pardon me!" the errant guest apologized in horrified tone. "I thought it was catsup."

As we might expect, a fair share of humor relates to sexual activities, since many of us bury deep our frustrated sexual desires. Such jokes usually center on the sexual act itself, perversion or the excretory functions. The telling of dirty jokes sometimes seems a minor national pastime.

But even the humor contained in a dirty joke shows a certain amount of strength and maturity—we are trying to find a civilized way to overcome an emotion we fear, rather than act on it and hurt someone or ourselves. We recognize reality and accept it even though we may not enjoy parts of it.

"Even in laughter the heart is sorrowful," the Bible states in Proverbs 14:13. But via laughter we may change sorrow into joy for the moment, or rage into calm. We do not need to analyze why we laugh, it is enough we feel a pleasure that lightens our spirit.

Our ability to laugh starts in the cradle, psychoanalysts say. If a baby is unable to smile, this foretells danger in his future emotional development. Dr. René Spitz conducted experiments showing the importance of a smile to the overall health of a baby. In hospitals he studied babies who had been abandoned by their mothers, taken care of by overworked, unloving nurses.

Referring to these studies, Dr. Grotjahn summed them up with the words: "The little faces of the babies who do not smile because they live without hope and faith convey more breath-taking tragedy than the human eye wishes to behold. Mother has left them. They seem to have seen death before they have tasted life. The faces show death and madness and lifelong schizophrenia. All these infants seem to express the intent to murder if given strength and the opportunity."

Follow-up studies showed that many of the "never-smiling" babies who had lost their mothers either developed a schizophrenic psychosis in later life or simply gave up and died in the hospital. Their facial expression in the first three months of life, with nary a smile, was correctly interpreted by observers; their fate could be predicted.

We might say that the smile is the first sign of love between baby and mother. If a mother cannot smile at her baby, even after it causes her an extra burden such as screaming for food, she may find an even angrier infant on her hands. One who now senses her irritation and anger rather than her love.

"The psychological relationship of mother and infant, in all its intimacy and expressed in the smiling response, is essential," Dr. Grotjahn warns. "The smile is the first expressive communication between two persons. The smile of the infant develops into the laughter of the baby."

And the laughter of the baby develops into the humor of the adult. As we make our way through a life that is sometimes harsh and difficult, we need, above all, to be able to laugh at ourselves and to know such laughter is a very precious psychic commodity.

Laughter offers an acceptable way to lessen our rage at feeling we are at the mercy of our two strongest impulses—the wish to get even with enemies (real and imagined) and the wish to enjoy more fully our sexual desires.

We often use the word *aggression* in connection with our angry feelings. Does the aggressive act always contain rage? Or are we able to be aggressive minus the feeling of rage?

2 🎵 The Difference between Rage and Aggression

At first Freud believed we possessed only one strong instinct—the sexual. He stated the sexual drive prevailed in our emotional development as we traveled through the oral, anal, phallic and genital "psychosexual" stages—ones that caused our deepest conflicts and aroused our angriest feelings.

At this time Freud theorized that our emotional conflicts arose from the clash between our conscious and unconscious erotic impulses and our conscious ego impulses, the latter mainly in the interest of self-preservation. Freud ignored all mention of "aggression" even though his mentor, Dr. Joseph Breuer, as early as 1895 wrote of "the aggressive instinct." Freud constantly spoke of "hate" and "sadism" but attributed them to the frustration of the sexual drive.

Then thirty years after he started his psychoanalytic work, Freud announced we possessed a second instinct that was equally as strong as the sexual—the aggressive drive, one that led to violent feelings of rage and fury. He also theorized that in early childhood our sexual and aggressive instincts were welded but, as we matured, they became more and more separate so we could distinguish between them and handle them more wisely.

Psychoanalysts have since discovered that what Freud called the "aggressive" impulse is not necessarily an evil, hostile one. Our aggression enables us to be successful at work, to enjoy our creativity, to enhance our ability to love others.

What does the word *aggression* mean? Past definitions have been murky and confusing. Again to quote *Webster's*, aggression is "an unprovoked attack or invasion." Over the centuries aggression has been connected to "evil" and "bad." It is also defined, however, as "full of enterprise and initiative; bold and active." This is a paradoxical point of view, as aggression is described both as an "unprovoked attack" but also an act that may be constructive and praiseworthy.

Aggression seems to have been a coverall word, encompassing many

19

feelings, acts and motives. It may be the cause of a violent or destructive act but it may also be the driving force beyond a successful career,
the painting of a masterpiece or the running for President of the United
States.

We might think of aggression, as some psychoanalysts have suggested, as a spectrum. At one end lies our destructive, angry wishes,
feelings and behavior—which at times may result in "hostile aggression." At the other end lies healthy aggression—the various ways in
which the emotion of raw aggression becomes converted into what we
might call the assertive spirit.

It is only when we act in cruel fashion, hurt someone else or ourselves physically or emotionally, that we call aggression "hostile" and
"dangerous." Rage is essentially a basic emotional response to some
thought or act (by someone else or ourselves) that causes anxiety
against which we try to defend ourselves.

This differs from "assertiveness," which is a quiet, confident way of
expressing ourselves even if we differ from others. Assertiveness brings
us self-esteem, not guilt at unrealistic anger. We feel we are in the right
and defend ourselves against injustice.

All of us possess the instinct or drive known as aggression. It provides
the physical and psychic energy that propels us toward the realization
of our aims. Those aims may be either destructive or peaceful. How we
handle the aggressive drive determines whether we injure or help ourselves and others.

Aggression may be either laudatory or despicable, lead us to em-
pathic acts or cruel ones. But without aggressive feelings to fuel us, we
could not succeed in transforming our wishes and fantasies into behavior. Behavior that gives us what we call a sense of identity as we shape
our lives.

If aggression leads us to a sense of respect and pride, our feeling of
self-love and self-confidence becomes strong. But if aggression leads us
to a lack of respect and low self-esteem, our sense of identity will remain weak and we may go through life unhappy and unfulfilled.

We are all capable of expressing the full range of aggression—its entire spectrum, if need be. If our life is threatened, we can kill to save
it—a necessary destructive act because self-preservation usually comes
first. Or if an attack is verbal, we can become aggressively verbal in return. We may fight with thoughts, words, gestures or facial expressions
of contempt, derision or hate as we try to defeat a hostile opponent.

Aggression may be used to gain vengeance on someone who has hurt us physically or emotionally. We may attack him with weapons or our hands or scathing words. We may plan to destroy him psychologically or wipe him out financially.

Aggression may also be used to climb the ladder to success. Or help make the world less dangerous by working for a deeper understanding of what has been called the "brotherhood of man."

The power of aggression may transform our dreams into realities, our wishes into acts. We need aggression to set in motion our daily life. We "wish to get up" in the morning and our aggressive impulse permits us to put this wish into a specific movement as we rise from bed. We wish to eat breakfast and our aggression fuels the act of eating. We wish to go to work and aggression propels us to drive the car or run to catch a train.

There is a world of difference between an aggressive thought or wish and an aggressive act. We may wish to hurt someone who has injured us but refrain from expressing our feelings in words or deeds as we control our emotions. We may act as though we forgive the offender, do not care about his behavior, wish to ignore it. Some may paralyze their use of the aggressive force because of emotional conflicts, too intimidated to act on their aggressive wishes and thoughts.

The physically paralyzed person is crippled in his use of aggression as an act but has access to his aggressive thoughts and wishes if he is not too frightened of them. He can also use aggression verbally.

During psychoanalysis each person is encouraged to face his rage, his hostile thoughts toward those he hates, both in the present and from childhood days. This is a necessary part of easing both depression and anxiety.

Ever since Freud described the aggressive instinct as one of our two strongest drives, a number of psychoanalysts have questioned whether aggression can be called an instinct, as Freud claimed. Dr. Phyllis Greenacre, for instance, called aggression "the expression of the life force of growth." Dr. Clara Thompson said she thought aggression "is not necessarily destructive at all" but that it "springs from an innate tendency to grow and master life, which seems characteristic of all living matter." She added, "Only when this life force is obstructed in its development do ingredients of anger, rage or hate become connected to it."

Dr. Gregory Rochlin focused on the defensive components of aggression as he stated, "When narcissism is threatened we are humiliated, our self-esteem is injured and aggression appears."

Though there seems no general agreement on an exact definition of aggression, there appears a growing acceptance of the idea that there exists this wide spectrum between the aggression used to express rage and the aggression that appears as a constructive "life force."

Over the centuries there has been one definition of aggression for men, another for women. If a man was described as aggressive, this implied he was appropriately masculine and successfully making his way in the world. A man without an aggressive manner was thought feminine, unmacho, not accorded much respect. For men, to be "aggressive" was laudable. For women, deplorable, unthinkable. Men thought of their aggression as desirable but decried the same attitude or act in women as destructive.

Poets and philosophers fully described this bias. St. Thomas Aquinas called woman a "misbegotten male." The word *misbegotten* means "wrongly or unlawfully begotten; specifically, born out of wedlock." In other words, woman was a "bastard." She was illegitimate, not up to the standards of a man.

The terrifying destructiveness of Medea stood as a male culture's perception of the dangerous and primitive nature of a woman's aggression. Medea's need for vengeance when her husband deserted her for another woman led her to murder their two sons. Clytemnestra was described as acting alien to the nature of woman, called "a woman with a man's will." With the aid of her lover, Aegisthus, she murdered her husband Agamemnon when he returned from the Trojan War, and she was consequently killed by their son Orestes. The denial in the past of a natural aggression in women has resulted in the assumption that rage and the display of violence by a woman is caused by mental derangement.

In the past woman has been forced by society to deny her right to express any form of aggression, from the hostile to the constructive, even though for men aggression was a word that covered a spectrum of sanctions. A man was praised for any show of aggressiveness, particularly in battle. A woman was condemned.

The cultural paranoia toward women that developed over the years is vividly described by Bram Dijkstra, in *Idols of Perversity: Fantasies of Feminine Evil in Fin-de-Siècle Culture.* Mr. Dijkstra, professor of comparative literature at the University of California, San Diego, mentions mermaids, vampires, sirens, and mythological women such as Circe, Lilith, Leda, Delilah, as representing demonic images of women as evil temptresses, bent on turning men away from their spiritual destiny and corrupting them with the pleasures of "sin."

In her review of the book in *The New York Times*, November 19, 1986, Michiko Kakutani points out that to men at the turn of the century, as Mr. Dijkstra states, "women were either virgins or whores, angels or devils, madonnas or vampires." This placed women "on an impossible pedestal," or doomed them to an unrealistic Satanic image.

But with the stirrings of the feminist movement, as woman rebelled against her appointed role "as a household nun," a male backlash occurred, according to Mr. Dijkstra. He wrote that men borrowed "evidence" from Darwin and other scientists to try to support the view of women as "voracious manhunters." The nurturing image of the Earth Mother was replaced by one of "an atavistic fertility machine, intent on removing man from the sphere of reason and pulling him down to a subhuman level."

It is little wonder that, until recently, a woman accepted man's derogatory attitude if she expressed the slightest show of aggression. She confused her capacity to use her assertiveness in a creative or otherwise self-fulfilling manner with what man and society labeled "hostile aggression."

To women, the slightest show of aggression has been misconstrued as rage. Women have felt guilty when they achieve in work, competing with men. Though women show what is essentially a healthy aggression, they think they are destructive.

Many women dare not feel angry even though they are justified in such anger, if they are exploited, demeaned or threatened. Anger is held unfeminine. A woman is expected to be only the nurturer, willing to deny all her right to assertiveness in behalf of husband and child.

If today's woman does not accept aggression as a spectrum of feelings, thoughts and acts, her life may be limited to servitude, fear and a hiding of her rage rather than fulfilling her capacity to love and to work, to enjoy living to the fullest. For her to understand more fully the role of assertiveness as it affects her daily experiences, she may have to become aware of how she has distorted her ideas as to what aggression means to her.

It is only in recent years that women, held back in certain respects by their fear of being thought "too aggressive," have taken steps toward achieving equality with men. Many women have been afraid to seek jobs held up to now only by men. Others fear appointment to top executive positions for which only men have been eligible. Women continue to feel guilty when they defeat men in the world of sports or political elections, as though they have no right to be the victor.

At the same time more and more women realize a society controlled by men has kept them from competing freely with men at work, creative efforts, taking part in governing the nation and writing its laws, judging its criminals. It has taken centuries for men to accept a show of assertiveness by women in its mildest form even when their aggressive impulses are modified by love, respect for and trust in others and themselves (a woman cannot trust or respect others until she trusts herself).

Since our aggressive and sexual desires are our two strongest, we tend to erect our most rocklike defenses against being aware of them if we are afraid of them. Many times when we feel an aggressive impulse, it is relegated at once to the unconscious part of our mind, often to become an unconscious fantasy that may control us. In the imaginations of those who murder the innocent, the fantasy has become so intense they cannot conquer it.

The power of fantasy may be seen in lesser intensity in most of us. A single woman, who turned down marriage proposals from man after man, insisted defiantly to a friend, "But I really *want* to get married." She "unreally" however did not wish to marry because she had the underlying fantasy that marriage would be dangerous, she would lose all right to shape and control her life, believing she must always give in to the man. She was unaware of the strength of this fantasy because it was hidden from her consciousness and seemed unreal, even though it was more powerful than her conscious wish to marry, of which she was aware.

Woman has denied her rage at men for exploiting her even more than she denied her sexual desire. Woman has had to pretend she feels no anger in order to exist in comparative safety in a world that has been, and still is, ruled by men.

"I had always been in a rage. I had been very angry since childhood. But what man would want an angry woman? The rage came out as charm." These were the words of Delphine Seyrig, the French actress who appeared in the film *Last Year at Marienbad*, when interviewed by *The New York Times* on July 31, 1976. Her thoughts echo the sentiments of countless women. Excessive charm, compliance and politeness may be defenses against a rage that reveals itself only in traumatic situations when all defenses break down. Most women control their anger though its subtle effect may be felt by husbands and children, not to mention society.

A woman of thirty-nine confessed to a friend that she took pride in acting like a sweet, unselfish human being who never raised her voice in anger or objected to anything anyone said or did, no matter how spiteful. "My reward is that everyone says I don't have an enemy in the world, that everyone loves me," she stated.

Then she added, as tears came to her eyes, "But I feel miserable all the time."

"Why?" asked the friend.

"I don't believe anyone," she said. "All the praise doesn't make me feel loved."

Her defense of sweetness and light, a defense assumed by many women, hid a deep rage that was promptly dismissed from awareness whenever she felt it. Through further understanding of herself, she became more capable of knowing she felt angry and of expressing anger when she felt justified. She also understood how she reenacted her behavior as a child to keep peace with an emotionally volatile mother and father. She now discovered a new sense of her own identity as she could be honest with herself.

Many a man or woman is apt to go through a typical day every so often, even if they do not step outside the house, when they experience fantasies of rage. Hatred is as much a part of life as love. Even toward those they love, people will occasionally harbor murderous wishes.

Psychoanalysts point out that anxiety is often the cover of repressed rage. And that fear creates anger. If we are afraid of someone we feel anger toward him. If a stranger with a gun holds us up, we first feel fear, followed by anger. If a fire breaks out in the room in which we sit, we flee in fear, then feel anger at the danger that has menaced us. Fear may be a response to any danger, a danger outside the self or a dangerous wish from within.

Some of our desires cause us fear and anger. A therapist may perceive a patient's fear of exposing his naked body to a partner with whom he enjoys sex as a defense against an infantile desire to exhibit himself.

Many of us carry from childhood fear of the intimidating mother and father, followed always by angry wishes to destroy them. Parents too often humiliate their children, make them feel inadequate, and this superior power keeps the child in a constant rage, though he conceals it as best he can from the parent. Some children, especially foster or adopted children, finally kill the parent they hate after they feel strong enough to combat the lifelong menace.

We may also hold a fear of our own anger. A woman of thirty told a friend, in commenting on a mutual friend, "I have to keep away from her. I get so angry at her narcissism, her inability to sympathize with anyone else but only to blame everyone for how she suffers, that I am afraid my anger will burst out at her one day and I'll feel dreadfully ashamed."

We need the ability to feel rage and fear in order to survive at times. Again, it is the degree of fear and rage that we feel that gives us a clue as to whether the rage or fear or both are justified or exist primarily in our fantasies. If justified, we need not be afraid of rage or fear, but if the product of fantasies, it is better to look at the fantasies so the fear and rage will ebb away.

An innocuous outlet for our buried rage is the reading of murder mysteries or watching murder scenes in the theater and on television. Or following real murders reported in the daily newspapers and news broadcasts. As both men and women take part vicariously in committing each murder, they gain some outlet for their hidden wishes to kill those who have offended them. Unconsciously they do not want the murderer caught because *they* would like to get away with murder. We might say that as we enjoy a murder mystery this means one murder—the one in our own hearts—goes uncommitted as the murderous wish finds a temporary outlet.

It is interesting that two of the most popular mystery writers have been British women—Agatha Christie and Josephine Tey—though there are also many other women mystery writers throughout the world. In this country Mary Higgins Clark has become famous for her murder mysteries, using a woman as the sleuth who tracks down the murderer. In all seven of her books, which have become best-sellers and films for movies and television, a woman discovers the killer. Ms. Clark says, "I write of women searching for the truth, trying to expose the wrongdoer, sensing evil when it is so deeply hidden others do not see it."

In each book the villain is a man. Ms. Clark explains, "The woman as villain is less universal. Woman hasn't the physical strength to be a killer, she seems less of a threat. I look for the universal. There aren't that many villainous women compared to men. Our psyche better accepts the threat and the deed of murder as coming from a strong male."

Perhaps more men than women are driven to the intensity of a rage that ends in murder. It appears so from the statistics. It may be that men's frustrations in the workplace—the greed to obtain more money—drives more men to murder. Greed certainly drives nation to war against nation and to kill the innocent.

Several psychoanalysts have noted that since the 1970s women's liberation movement their women patients have revealed more dreams constructed around fantasies of rage. As women feel more entitled to acknowledge their murderous anger it finds freer expression in dreams, if not acts. Joseph Katz, in his recent book *Dreams Are Your Truest Friends*, says that women's dreams are "clearly changing, becoming less submissive, and there is less acting the role of the helpless, fearful victim destined to suffer endless humiliation with its inevitable build-up of anger."

Another reason woman has feared to express assertiveness is that she has been so angry at men for their exploitation of her that she fears hostility will emerge, rather than healthy aggression. She has not dared examine the difference between her natural desire to assert herself—to want to achieve success, to be creative, to earn as much as a man for the same work, and to speak her mind as freely—as contrasted with her natural desire to hurt man because he has made her suffer in so many ways.

Women have to be aware, however, that they do not seek power, success and wealth at the expense of ignoring their emotional and sexual needs. As well as ignoring the needs of a man they love. Psychoanalysts advise that if a woman's drive for achievement overpowers her ability to think of others who depend on her for love, she would do well to examine her envy of men, her wish to be like a man. Many women are still dominated by the childish fantasy that if only they had been born a boy, life would be far more pleasurable. Such a wish is not surprising in view of women's low status in society through the ages. That status can only enhance her natural fantasy that if she were born a boy, all avenues open to man would be available to her.

Like men, women too may possess the erroneous fantasy that with a sense of power comes happiness and self-esteem. As if power, success and wealth, though they temporarily do in a superficial way, bring happiness. Power does, however, automatically evoke the feeling, "I am good, I am loved and I did it all myself. I don't need anyone—man or woman—I am complete within myself."

Both men and women may view power as protection against needing to be dependent on others who may betray or fail to protect. If you are powerful enough, famous enough, successful enough, rich enough, you fantasy that you are beyond any hurt mortal man can inflict, sufficient unto yourself.

Women's fear of displaying aggression in a constructive way has hindered their struggle to achieve full liberation. A liberation that includes deeper understanding of themselves, as well as enhancing their capacity to love, to cherish a family and to work more creatively.

As a forty-two-year-old woman, assistant to the president of a large advertising agency, said, "I want to be able to do my work effectively, see my adolescent son and daughter and husband at night and weekends, and feel no guilt."

She has entered a new world—a world that permits her to seek a career in whatever field she wishes (with some exceptions that still bar women) even though she may be mother and wife. But she has to be emotionally ready to do this. She must not feel angry at herself, then guilty, at the thought of neglecting her home or, when at work, depriving a man of a job.

The false belief that "a woman's work is never done" has been used to confine women to the home. But as Sigourney Weaver, well-known actress, star of the film *Aliens,* said when interviewed on Channel 5 in New York on October 31, 1986, "You *can* have it all—but you have to be well-organized." She added that she wanted to continue her successful career in films and on the stage, be a wife and mother, and expected to be happy in all these areas.

Such is the new philosophy of a growing number of women. A philosophy that can only bring increased happiness if they can accept that assertiveness is not hostile aggression. Assertiveness is the constructive expression of a natural drive that exists to be used either destructively or constructively.

Women's hard-fought freedoms have brought new challenges as well as new conflicts as women express themselves, or fail to express themselves, in what they think of as "aggressive ways." For instance, a thirty-year-old woman executive in an advertising agency, married to a lawyer, admitted to her sister, "I'm afraid to tell my husband I want more privacy at home. I need a separate room in which to sit quietly and think, on weekends. About ad campaigns. Or maybe to write a short story if I feel like it."

"Why can't you tell him?" her sister asked.

"He'll think I want him out of the way and he'll feel hurt and angry."

"Do you believe if you have the courage to assert your feelings about wishing to be creative he will respond as though it were an attack on him?" her sister said incredulously.

The woman replied lamely, "I try to put his feelings first."

"Your interests are equal to his," her sister said. "You're entitled to privacy as much as he is. Why don't you think you are?"

The woman, older than her sister by ten years, said, almost apologetically, "Mother brought me up to think of the man's needs first and I still do. It's like her voice is still inside me. Maybe by the time you were a teenager, she had become more of a liberated woman."

Her sister said thoughtfully, "You are entitled to a small space of your own where you can think in quiet any time you wish. Your home has plenty of rooms. Stop punishing yourself and stand up for your rights."

After her sister left, the woman thought about what she advised. That night she told her husband she planned to use a small room on the second floor as a den where she could work on weekends and in the evening, away from distractions. She expected him to object. To her amazement he kissed her, said, "I'm sorry I didn't think of it first."

This woman had been afraid to assert what certainly was her right, confusing it with hostile aggression. Unfortunately, this often occurs in the lives of many women as they restrain their wish to get ahead in careers, fearing they are too aggressive, believing such aggression to be spurred by hate rather than the normal desire to be productive, creative and contribute to society. They *are* aggressive but healthily so, yet cannot tolerate the aggressive feelings. In some instances the wish to be productive is accompanied by envy of men and hate for them because of past exploitation. This causes the women to fear their aggressiveness.

There are many ways aggression in women may easily be appropriately expressed without becoming a destructive act if they accept the difference between aggression as natural assertion and aggression as a wish to hurt or to destroy. It lies however within the individual woman, so that the road ahead may prove less rocky, to know herself better so she can take charge of her life.

Her constructive, aggressive feelings will prevail over her destructive hostile ones as she can face and accept those hurts of the past that may be causing her to repress her rage and feel guilty. Once she accepts buried anger and its cause, she can use the energy tied up in repressing her rage for love, creativity, friendship, social causes, whatever she wills.

The liberation of women in many areas has brought new challenges as women keep from expressing themselves in destructive ways and express themselves more in constructive ways. Women also have to fight the misinterpretation of their use of aggression in acceptable form. For instance, when someone says in contempt, "Now *there's* an aggressive woman," the adjective often has not been fairly used. There is nothing to be censored when a woman appears assertively aggressive. "Hostile" is another matter. Aggression may mean quiet assertion based on the conviction it is a woman's right to speak up and be heard. Or defend herself when she is verbally demeaned or exploited.

If a woman has confidence in herself she can use her new freedoms in enhancing, meaningful ways. She can "choose" instead of being driven. She can say "no" when she feels in the right instead of trying to placate or please.

It will take women time to make peace with their aggressive wishes and accept them as natural. And also to convince men it is to the advantage of both men and women that women accept the right to be constructively assertive so they can feel self-esteem, for this means they will raise happier children.

The right to assertiveness has been a long time coming to women. The past centuries have not granted women parity with men in most areas of living. This century does not grant it to most women of the world.

Perhaps civilization can move only so fast in its slothlike stride toward equality for women. But the greater the number of women able to use their assertive spirit, the faster the achievement of equality not only for them but for everyone.

Freedom, in whatever measure, is always contagious. The freedom of a woman to feel equal to a man in all spheres of life—economic, sexual, political and social—is her long overdue inalienable right.

Hopefully, more and more women will accept this right to a place on the spectrum of aggression where "assertiveness" in their own behalf in the workplace, the home and the national and world scenes will be recognized as equal to man's use of aggression in the same spheres.

Their deserved equality will free women from feeling the hostile aggression that is the natural result of unfair treatment. The equality will encourage women to use assertiveness in ways that will profit not only their existence but all those to whom they are close. A woman will feel true partners with a man, no longer an enemy. She will give up the war between the sexes, in which she has killed not with a sword but the look or the word. The very phrase "male chauvinist pig" tells as much about the woman who hurls it in fury as the exploiting male at whom it is directed.

Over the centuries men and women have envied each other for the unique qualities each possesses. Psychoanalysts make the point that men envy women because a man cannot give birth to a child, perhaps the greatest achievement of a human being, for civilization cannot continue unless babies are born. But women need men for the birth of a baby—each gender contributes.

Women have envied men their power, symbolically represented by the penis. Women have also envied men for the many rights they have assumed are theirs alone, denying them to women, rationalizing they are inferior in mind, body and earning power.

How men shape their aggressive force differs from the way women do. Men are not supposed to show any sign of weakness when they are hurt and angry. One of the most, if not the most moving moment in the World's Series of 1986 occurred when, in the sixth game, the Mets suddenly snatched victory from what looked like victory for their opponents. All the players left the field except Wade Boggs, third baseman for the defeated Bostonians, who had despondently abandoned their dugout.

Boggs, however, remained alone, seated, his eyes on the empty field as though unable to face what, for him, was the tragic end. He had worked hard during the year, had become the batting champion of the American League. And as he sat there, the darkness descending, the camera focused on his handsome face. Tears formed in his eyes, then slowly a few tears trickled down his cheeks as he sat immobile, saddened beyond words. The Mets, as Boggs feared, went on to win the seventh game of the Series.

Boggs's electric scene was described the next day by reporters in newspapers and on television. One columnist said it was the moment he would remember above all others. A photograph of that moment of grief appeared in the newspaper. The impact was strong because the mighty hitters of the baseball world, among the most powerful of athletes, are not supposed to cry, especially in public. But Boggs's grief was so overwhelming he had been unable to move from his wooden seat.

Society's expectations that men never show tears means that men are expected to be more "nonhuman" than women. Men are supposed to repress their grief, their sorrow and the rage that always is part of grief— yet when we are deprived of something, we automatically wish to cry, as we did when a baby.

An interesting description of the difference between men and women and the aggressive spirit was presented in a course titled "Men, Women and Aggression," given by former Lieutenant Colonel Faris R. Kirkland of the United States Army (1972 to 1980). Colonel Kirkland is now a lecturer in the Department of History at Bryn Mawr College, Bryn Mawr, Pennsylvania.

He summed up the course, explaining, "The fundamental social observation is that members of both sexes are capable of hostile feelings and violent behavior." He added, "Men behave violently more often in familial and social life and have a near-monopoly on war."

He attributed this to the "fundamental psychiatric observation that
male humans undergo relatively more difficult processes of individuation than do females, and therefore generate and repress more hostility." He explained that "individuation" refers to the emotional process
involved in separating from the mother in the earlier years of life.

He said further: "Women fight to protect themselves, people vital to
them and their nests. Men are promiscuous fighters; they will fight over
remote abstractions. I concluded provisionally that war is therefore a
man's game and that women humor them by letting them play it."

In a front-page story in *The New York Times* on August 26, 1986,
Richard Halloran wrote from Washington that during the thirteen years
since the United States ended the draft and returned to volunteer military service, women, blacks and "young married persons" have "transformed the nation's armed forces."

From World War II until 1973 when conscription ended, the services
were male preserves dominated by white officers and noncommissioned
officers, and the lower ranks were principally single young men. But
today three changes have reached into every corner of military life,
Halloran reported: (1) The armed forces, especially the Army, have
carried racial integration further than most American institutions. (2)
With women, the armed forces have embarked on an ambitious experiment that has raised moral, political and practical questions. Even so,
according to Carolyn Becraft of the Women's Equity Action League,
"The United States is far and away ahead of other nations in making
use of women in the military." (3) One-third of lower ranking enlisted
soldiers, sailors, airmen and marines are married and this has resulted
in marked changes in service camaraderie, discipline and housing.
Coping with the needs of young families, says an Army white paper, has
become "an institutional imperative."

The presence of women has caused greater changes in military life
than nuclear weapons have, according to General John W. Vessey Jr.,
former chairman of the Joint Chiefs of Staff. "We've taken a male institution in a very short period and turned it into a coed institution, and
it has been a traumatic exercise for us."

Among the obvious changes, women require separate living quarters,
different sizes and shapes in clothing, different standards for physical
training and different medical services. There is also the matter of sex,
Halloran pointed out in his story. He wrote, "Commanders worry about
men and women distracting each other on duty. Dating, or what military people call 'fraternization,' has led to new rules. That has led to

complicated administrative problems when two members of the service marry, when women in the military become pregnant and when a member of the service is a single parent."

Most perplexing of all has been "defining the role of women in combat, an issue far from decided," Halloran said. "Underlying this are cultural questions: the place of women in Western civilization; the instinct to preserve women to bear children; and concepts of chivalry that date back to the Middle Ages."

The armed forces have edged closer to placing women where they could find themselves in combat. The first women to serve in crews controlling Minuteman 2 nuclear missiles descended to two command capsules sixty-five feet underground at Whiteman Air Force Base in Montana on March 25, 1986. In a nuclear war, women in such capsules would be prime targets and might be among the first ordered to fire. Army women drive trucks that could go close to combat zones and Navy women are aboard support ships that could be targets in a conflict. Women may not carry rifles on offensive operations, serve aboard warships or fly war planes.

Today, 20 percent of the 2,100,000 people in the armed forces are women. They comprise 11.9 percent of the Air Force, which has a large support structure. All but five of 230 enlisted job classifications are open to women. In the Army, which also has a large support force, 10.3 percent of the soldiers are women. Of 351 military occupational specialties, 302 are open to women. In the Navy, 9.3 percent of the sailors are women. The Marine Corps, for which the Navy provides most of the support force, has 4.9 percent women.

Many officers report women miss fewer days on duty, even with menstruation or pregnancy, are less often absent without leave, and get into less trouble with drinking or drugs, Halloran reports. Socially, the services forbid commissioned officers to date enlisted persons. Whatever the strictures, a steady increase in marriages between members of the services has occurred and complicates the transfers common to military life.

Women who are noncommissioned officers said their greatest problem has been gaining acceptance by men, either as superiors or subordinates. The women reported this lack of acceptance was a more frequent form of sexual harassment than overt advances. Getting male subordinates to follow orders has at times been difficult. Petty Officer First Class Carol L. Denson told Halloran, "Some of the men are afraid of having women in positions of authority. It's hard to assert your authority because the men will go around you to a male superior and he'll take their side."

A group of women veterans of the war in Vietnam has announced plans to place a bronze statue of an American military nurse on the grounds of the Vietnam Veterans Memorial on the Mall in Washington, DC. Eight women's names are among the 58,132 Vietnam war dead on the monument's long panels of black granite. About three million American military men and seven to ten thousand women, most of them nurses or other medical service workers, served in Vietnam.

The proposed statue has gained widespread support "because there were so many women in Vietnam and because the suffering and contributions of women have too often been overlooked in American life," said John Wheeler, chairman of the memorial fund. There will be a million-dollar drive for the women's memorial. Roger M. Brodin of Minneapolis has sculpted a two-foot model of the proposed statue, showing a young woman in fatigues and combat boots with a stethoscope around her neck and a helmet in her hands.

It is not, however, in actual battle with other nations but in quiet resolution of conflicts within the self that both men and women will find the courage and strength to put aside the prejudices of centuries that have enslaved women and inevitably produced deep rage. Only then will they reach new heights in bringing peace to the world and the nation. But first there must be felt that emotional freedom that leads to self-esteem in the fullest sense.

The distinction between assertive aggression and hostile aggression must be clearly recognized and dealt with. This distinction was aptly described by center fielder Rickey Henderson, a leading base stealer and home-run hitter on the New York Yankees. He was labeled by reporters during the season of 1986 as "arrogant" in the way he stole bases.

He told a reporter in defense, "I don't see my base stealing as an arrogance. I see it as aggressiveness." He was speaking of aggression as assertion, used in the "good" sense, not destructive hostility.

There is a vast difference between rage that is realistic and justified and rage that is unrealistic and not justified. When rage is justified, we should not fear expressing it in behalf of our own rights. But if we constantly feel angry not in a justified manner but because of vengeful fantasies of the past, we should carefully examine our wishes and feelings.

3 🎧 Where Rage Starts

Aggression may develop in a number of ways, influencing later behavior. What determines the manner in which aggression may take different forms?

Where does rage begin? Rage may be part of the aggressive drive that starts prenatally in the unborn child if something goes awry within the mother, says Dr. Wilfred Gaylin. He wrote in *The Rage Within: Anger in Modern Life* that the "scream of a baby" contains rage that "resembles the rage of a wounded animal."

He further pointed out that young, very emotionally disturbed parents have killed their babies and young children because they "could not stand the screaming." The screams reminded them, no doubt, of their own cry for help and murderous feelings as babies when they felt cold, hungry, wet, neglected (and were probably hit violently by their parents at such times).

Some psychoanalysts believe that Joel Steinberg destroyed his adopted daughter Lisa when she acted in ways that reminded him of the hated child in himself. He told Hedda Nussbaum that he administered the fatal blow to Lisa's head because she kept "staring" at him. Perhaps this was the way his mother stared at him as a child when he misbehaved, or he stared at her when she hurt him.

Dr. Gregory Rochlin explains in *The Masculine Dilemma* that during the early development of a child, both boys and girls "at first naturally find their definition through the wish to be like their mothers." The boy soon wishes however to abandon this aim when he becomes aware of his father and tries to imitate him. If he continues to wish to be feminine, this indicates a reaction to masculinity that unconsciously has been prohibited (if a mother hates the father, for instance, the boy will not wish to be like his father).

Rochlin explains this reaction is "based on an earlier-seated identification with his mother that has been prolonged." He adds that the conscious aim of requiring femininity when masculinity is too anxiety provoking "is to take on the safer, feminine role." He also emphasizes that "a mother conveys her conflicts to her child."

He points out that early in masculine development, a boy's narcissism is used in the service of "narcissism"—we are all narcissistic as children, believe the world revolves around us and our parents are present only to serve our needs. Rochlin says that a boy's narcissism, "uniquely vulnerable, readily mobilizes aggression to defend it. This is what a boy does about his aggression."

He adds, "The more vulnerable masculine narcissism seems, the more readily is aggression mobilized in its defense. Whether the aggressive defenses are expressed as impotent rages or become highly sophisticated intellectual pursuits naturally depends on circumstance, the level of developed maturity possible, and the degree to which self-curbs or aggression turned on oneself develops."

At first Freud believed, as he put it, that the cause of man's inner rage "lies in sexual experiences of infancy, usually commonplace in themselves," but easily intensified and warped if parents did not offer loving care. He warned against violence in the home or unwarranted "sexual acting out" on the part of parents who walked around naked in front of the growing child or allowed him at any time from birth on to witness them in sexual intercourse (this arouses in the child the fantasy that sex is a violent act as he pictures the father attacking the mother). These become "sexual traumas of childhood," which the child carries with him into adulthood as they assume more and more control over his sexual and aggressive life.

Freud commented, "We shall indeed be . . . the richer . . . for directing our attention to these most significant after-effects of infantile impressions which have hitherto been so grossly neglected."

The ways in which children express aggression are influenced by how their parents express aggression. Some children have loving, nurturing mothers and grow up able to assert themselves quietly, with little need to hide deep rage or construct fantasies of revenge. Others possess mothers who are uncaring, or overpossessive, or unable to control their rage when the child misbehaves; the child is apt to imitate in adulthood the way he was treated in earlier years.

How a mother reacts to a baby tells how she probably will react throughout the child's development. The mother is able to show love, patience and an understanding of the baby's needs if she has, for the most part, wanted the child, though ambivalence is always present to some degree. If she resents the child as a burden, did not wish to bear him, she is likely to display hatred, impatience and neglect.

The history of how children were treated through the ages "is a nightmare from which we have only recently begun to awaken," says Lloyd DeMause, founder of the International Psychohistorical Associa-

tion and editor of and contributor to *The History of Childhood*. Headlines in our daily newspapers show how prevalent brutal child abuse still
is throughout our nation.

DeMause comments that the brutality of parents is "a replaying of
their battered childhood at the hands of parents." They ask the child
to be their own good parents, give them the mothering they never had,
and when the child inevitably fails, they punish him as they once
wished to punish their punitive parents.

"Once born, the child becomes the mother and father's own parent,
in either positive or negative aspect, totally out of keeping with the
child's actual age," says DeMause. "It is the child's function, the parents believe, to reduce the adult's pressing anxieties; the child acts as
the adult's defense."

Child abuse thus reflects both the rage of the parent at the child
(mirroring how the parent was treated as a child) and the rage of the
child at being struck violently or sexually molested or neglected. We
might venture the guess that all the drug addicts in our nation had
childhoods that in some way aroused their rage—they felt more hatred
than love in their parents. The addict emotionally still remains the unhappy, angry child.

Probably no person in the history of mankind has been raised as a
child with a minimum of anger in the house, says DeMause. But at least
we are starting to realize how vital it is for a child to be treated gently,
nurtured with love and understanding. The high rate of child abuse in
this country alone, a country that claims to be fairly civilized, shows
how far we need to go to further the early care of children.

If Adam and Eve had been understanding parents they never would
have produced a son who became a murderer (and of his brother). Sibling rivalry ran high in the world's reported first family. Man's real task
has been not to acquire money but to conquer the rage in himself that
is not justifiable but arises out of childhood hate, jealousy and the wish
to be the one and only.

It is not however alone the feeling of rage at something that threatens but the intensity of the buried feelings of rage that over the years
becomes destructive. Such intensity usually stems from our childhood
fantasies that emerged as defense against what we believed to be rejection and mistreatment by parents. Fantasy piled on fantasy dealing with
revenge adds up to a high degree of rage.

A thirty-three-year-old man, a successful lawyer, went into analysis
realizing he felt far too much anger at his wife and daughter. It took

him months before he felt safe enough with the analyst to say in anger, "My damned father used to call me a little stinker and told me I would never amount to anything because my marks in school were too low. And my cowardly mother would never defend me, just sat there and seemed to agree with him."

He had never fought back, needing his father's love and support, but his anger simmered over the years. When he started to express it to his wife and daughter, he realized he needed help in understanding why he could lose his temper at them but never at his father.

We all carry from childhood a certain degree of rage we try to keep hidden from ourselves, as well as those we love, who have been our caretakers. As Dr. Gaylin reminds us, "Rivalry in the oedipal situation is one in which the child never wins. The boy, in competing with his father for the love of his mother, must eliminate the father. But to destroy the father is terrifying to the child, who recognizes his own impotence and understands that his survival depends on the goodwill, the resources and the strengths of that parent."

The oedipal plight is even more difficult for a girl, he believes, "for in competing for her father she must displace that ultimate symbol of nurture in childhood, the mother. To lose the competition with the parent is to reaffirm your helpless state as a child. To win the competition is even more dreadful, for firmly fixed in one's unconscious self-image is the awareness of one's limited resources and one's dependence on the parental figure. To have destroyed that parental figure is a hollow victory indeed, for it is shattering the very vessel that keeps one afloat."

A woman of forty-three, two years into psychoanalysis, was finally able to confess to her analyst, "As I grew up I was torn between deep hate and deep love for my mother. I adored my handsome father, wanted him all to myself but had to hide this not only from my parents but myself. I knew at times I loathed my mother but never felt anything but love for my father even though he could be mean and sarcastic, wipe me out for the moment."

In analysis she became more aware of her love for her mother and her hate for her father when she realized, as Freud said, "No love is pure." Especially that of a child for a parent.

The love-hate for a sibling is another confusing conflict, often arousing much anxiety. Every child with a brother or sister or both has the fantasy, at first conscious, then unconscious, of destroying the sibling to get full possession of the mother and father's love.

A three-year-old boy, staring at his newborn brother, instructed his mother, "Take him away. I don't want him in the house." His mother assured him, "You'll learn to love him as you help him grow up." He replied angrily, "Never!" But slowly he learned to tolerate, then become friends with, then love his little brother, all wishes to destroy now consigned to the storehouse of memories we call the unconscious.

Dr. Gaylin explains that one reason the death of a sibling, particularly during the survivor's adolescence, "is so devastating a blow" lies in the fact that during the past, since the sibling has so often been "wished" dead, and since to the unconscious, "wishing *can* make it so," the burden of guilt may be a heavy one and apt to be carried through a lifetime unless faced consciously.

One convenient device for expressing anger while preserving caution, Dr. Gaylin points out, "is to disguise the anger, to offer the assault in the form of something else." He calls "sarcasm" a particularly deprecating way of being funny; it is at the same time a funny way of being deprecating. Sarcasm defies retaliation with the implication that to take umbrage is a sign of inadequacy, a lack of humor, "What's the matter—can't you take a joke?" Dr. Gaylin describes sarcasm as an adolescent form of humor "which most of us fortunately outgrow by the time we become adults."

Anger is described as "a signal, and one worth listening to," by Harriet Goldhor Lerner, PhD, in her best-selling book, *The Dance of Anger*. She explains, "Our anger may be a message that we are being hurt, that our rights are being violated, that our needs or wants are not being adequately met, or simply that something is not right, . . . that too much of our self—our beliefs, values, desires, or ambitions—is being compromised in a relationship."

She believes that "just as physical pain tells us to take our hand off the hot stove, the pain of our anger preserves the very integrity of our self. Our anger can motivate us to say 'no' to the ways in which we are defined by others and 'yes' to the dictates of our inner self."

It is a vicious circle—parents expect children to be perfect and children expect parents to be perfect. Dr. W. Hugh Misseldine in *Your Inner Child of the Past* points out that "the perfectionist person continues the downgrading-striving cycle which the child he once was *had* to accept from his parents as the way of life."

The need to be perfect is created in the child by "persistent parental demand, expressed in terms of what was expected from the child," Mis-

seldine says. Usually his behavior and development "had to be more ad-
vanced and more mature than the child could comfortably achieve at
the moment."

A man of thirty-two, as he lay on the couch, told his analyst, "If I
didn't behave perfectly as a child, as a growing boy and as an adolescent, my father would sneer, 'You're such a dummy.' Or 'When will you
grow up?' He was a broker on Wall Street and he would come home and
tell us how much money he made that day. He would boast, 'I never
make a mistake on stocks.'"

A woman of twenty-six, talking to her analyst, said of her mother,
"If I didn't always behave like a quiet, perfect little lady my mother
would look at me scornfully and say, 'When *will* you grow up so I don't
have to be ashamed of you?'" The woman added, "I realize now that
my mother's mother, my rigid grandmother, talked to her just like that
when *she* was a little girl. So I forgive my mother. I don't have to be
that little girl any longer. I can understand my mother made unreal demands on me based on how she was brought up."

Children need, and seek, according to Dr. Misseldine, "the affec-
tionate acceptance of themselves through their efforts to please their
parents." But perfectionist parents tend to withhold acceptance of the
child unless he reaches continuous top performance. Sometimes however even if the child becomes adept at any task, from moving his bow-
els to using correct table manners or achieving good grades, the parent
will not give full approval. Instead, he will urge the child to "do better."
The child will then feel belittled, anxious about his performances and
abilities. He will possess little confidence in himself no matter how high
his future accomplishments.

Some perfectionist parents may use punishment or try to coerce the
child with bribery. One mother, each time she put her one-year-old son
on the toilet, trying to "civilize him," as she described it, would wave
a candy bar in front of his nose and say, "After you've performed for
mommy, you can have this delicious chocolate."

Dr. Misseldine warns it is sometimes difficult as an adult to recognize
your own demands for perfection. The early demands of a parent,
which would explain either why you must drive yourself trying to find
perfection or feel inferior and worthless, become lost in the limbo of
the unconscious.

Only when we recognize the subtlety and daily current repetition of
the belittling parental words in our early life that now extend into every
aspect of our living from study to play can we start to understand how

we acquired our basic dissatisfaction with ourselves, Dr. Misseldine points out. He adds, "If you have continued to apply these same belittling expressions to whatever you do, you are undermining yourself."

To the parent, his orders to the child appear based on love and concern for the child's welfare. Often the parent is not aware that many of his commands are aimed at trying to make up for his own past deprivations.

A mother told her eight-year-old daughter, "My mother died when I was only four years old and I don't want you to feel you have no emotional anchor. I want the very best for you. I want you to *be* the very best." She was laying the ground for her daughter's unhappiness in the years to come as the daughter pushed herself to be the very best child ever conceived. She was doomed to fall short of such perfection, never felt comfortable within as an adult.

A few children will passively resist the parent, show an attitude of "I don't care if I don't please you. It's more important that I proceed at my own stupid pace." Unconsciously they are showing their anger at the parent. Such children may become apathetic adults who cannot seem to finish anything they start. They seldom achieve top jobs, they are not creative, but "passive," still unconsciously resisting the tyrant parent.

The person who demands perfection of himself and/or others usually finds it difficult to get along easily with those to whom he becomes intimate, wishes to love. Because he forever strives to achieve, his constant self-belittling mitigates against the acceptance of his own limits or accepting the limits of others. Such acceptance is needed for a lasting love relationship.

The perfectionist person prefers to seek areas in which his performance is measurable, Dr. Misseldine says, such as work, athletic contests and social status. He continues the striving started "at home" as a child, "pursuing the will-o'-the-wisp promise of eventual full acceptance. He tends to view life as participation in a race and to feel the intimate and mutual interchange of a close relationship as too binding and distracting, something which keeps him from running at full speed."

The loving acceptance of a wife or sweetheart is, he feels, nothing compared to what he will possess if he "succeeds in winning the race— 'does better.'" Any obstacle that impedes his progress, such as taking time out to enjoy sex or affection or companionship makes him afraid he will lose the prize he has sought since childhood, the promise of full

acceptance held out by his mother and father. This goal blots out the
rest of living. "Performance" rather than caring about someone else,
sexuality or tenderness go by the board. All he seeks is better and better
"performance" in work, in "getting ahead" socially and monetarily.

Such a man will feel his lack of sexual potency as a crushing blow.
If the woman does not respond "perfectly" to him, he blames himself.
A woman perfectionist also seeks performance at any cost. Her failure
or the man's in achieving orgasms results in depression, the feeling she
is worthless, as she sinks into the fantasy that she is an omnipotent
child who must be perfect.

Such an attitude easily destroys a marriage or keeps the perfectionist
from finding someone to live with. He seeks the "perfect" mate, someone without flaws—such a person does not exist. Sometimes the perfectionist will delay marrying for years or give up trying to achieve
closeness with someone of the opposite sex.

If he does marry, he will not enjoy his partner or his own feelings.
He will continue to demand perfection of both. Anything less than
"perfect" arouses his childhood anxiety and fear of losing the love of his
mother and father and this enrages him and brings out the very early
emotions of anger he felt as a child at such impossible demands.

One twenty-seven-year-old woman who married a perfectionist (per-
fectionists tend to marry nonperfectionists, reflecting their unconscious
wish to be nonperfect as a child), told her closest friend, who had been
married happily for seven years, "Jim gets violently upset, sometimes
screams at me, if I don't cook the chicken to perfection the way he likes
it. Not too well done, not undercooked. And he can't stand it if the
laundry does not use exactly the right amount of starch in his shirts."

She sighed, added, "I never saw such a temperamental man. I don't
know how much longer I can stand it." After another six months, she
called her friend, said sadly, "I've moved out of the house. I'm getting
a divorce."

The rage of such a husband had accumulated over the years; he relieved himself of some of it as he exploded at his wife in a way he formerly dared not indulge in at the mother and father of infancy. He was
able to show his wife the emotions he felt as a child but dared not express at parents who expected the impossible of him.

A thirty-seven-year-old man, an executive in a large New York advertising agency, after eight months on the couch, confessed to his analyst, "When I was a boy of seven or eight, I felt furious at my mother

and father. They were terribly rigid parents. One day I asked them for a set of boxing gloves and they bought two basketballs I could tie to the rafters in the cellar. I marked one of them 'mother' and the other 'father' and punched away alternately at the balls. That way I got out some of my fury at their rigidity and impossible demands."

Thus the start of buried rage in our lives as children. It can become rage of varied degrees, depending on how deeply we felt hurt at the hands of unwise, unloving, sometimes cruel parents.

Most of us fortunately escape the parent who turns violent when the child does not meet his demands for perfectionism. If violence is combined with cruelty, if physical or sexual abuse is inflicted on the child on whom demands are made to be perfect, then the child, as adult, may suffer deeply from a torrential rage that eventually screams for release, may lead to murder or suicide or multiple personalities or schizophrenia and paranoia.

Then there is the rage of adolescents when parents break up or those who know their parents cheat on each other, causing an undercurrent of deceit in the family. The parent not only betrays his marital partner but his children, they feel. This living of two lives by a parent also affects the child's view of marriage and he is apt to repeat the same behavior in his marriage.

This was discussed on Phil Donahue's program on "How Marital Infidelity Affects Children," which appeared on February 15, 1989. Donahue commented, "It's legal to have a shrink in such instances. How people get through life without one, I don't know." He also said when parents are not faithful to each other "they have no understanding of the damage done to children. The parent is being a selfish child himself."

A well-known psychoanalyst, Dr. Henri Parens, who has studied the aggression of early childhood, points out that aggression "*develops*, it is not just a given.*" Because our aggressive feelings are developmental, "this means we can find ways of enhancing that aspect of aggression we value and lessen that which causes us harm and hardship," he states in his paper, "Toward a Reformulation of the Theory of Aggression and Its Implications for Child Development Theory," which appears in *Psychoanalysis: The Vital Issues*, Volume I, edited by Dr. John Gedo and Dr. George H. Pollock.

The current effort is "to develop a strategy for preventing the development of excessive hostility in children," Parens says. He calls "the internalization of maternal dictates" the first cause of ambivalence, which leads to aggressive feelings, then guilt in the child. The neutralization of aggression begins when, during the last half of the first year of life, the child's ego begins to function and he can experience anxiety, a wish, the intention of an act. The principal impetus is the child's "transient wish to destroy his occasionally too frustrating mother," Parens explains. The hostile destructiveness of the child becomes mobilized by frustration, is attached to the mother and becomes invested in her.

Parens observed children from four to six months of age as well as later in their development. He found signs in their behavior that he says "challenged the classical psychoanalytic view that all aggression is in origin inherently destructive."

Referring to the aggressive drive as "the umbrella word for the drive as one entity," he declares: "The human child is *not born with* an ever-replenishing load of hostility that he/she must discharge. Rather, the child is born with a ready-to-function mechanism that will *transform aggression into hostile destructiveness.*" He describes the basic trends of the drive as "nondestructive aggression, nonaffective destructiveness and hostile destructiveness."

Because of its "indelibility and omnipresent influence," the hostile destructiveness invested in the earliest person known, the mother, and subsequent representations of the self, becomes the fountainhead of hostility in the psyche, he maintains. He suggests, "This is how hostile destructiveness becomes *automatized* in the psyche and gives the clinical impression of being an instinctual drive." (In other words, we may trace the roots of the wish to murder, literally and implied, in the rage of a child toward the mother.)

While the potential mobilization of hostile destructiveness is part of every child's psychic apparatus and constitutional endowment, its actual mobilization and accumulation in the psyche "derive from the child's experiences" with his parents, Parens concludes. He calls the most common and largest source of hostile destructiveness "the vicissitudes of libidinal [love] object relations."

He believes, therefore, "we ought to look at how parents rear their children, and to explore ways by which their children, and in consequence, society, can be better protected against the development of excessive hostility." He urges that children be protected "from too *frequent and too prolonged* emotional pain," which means there is a "need for empathy in parents." He makes a plea for the education of parents in schools, from kindergarten through the last year of high school, to help mothers and fathers, teachers and caretakers of children learn more about the "nurturing environment" children require.

Parens's findings have provided more understanding of the way hostile destructiveness develops and the ways children discharge it, both in wishes and acts. He also has shown the character of the contribution of aggression to conflicts, adaptation and psychic development. For instance, a little girl has an inborn need to assert herself in order to master her emotions and the environment as she strives to overcome obstacles that stand in the way of her wishes and goals.

At the age of four months, she starts to explore her body and the world around her with her mouth (not only food but toys go into it) and her fingers. She later uses her aggressive force to talk, to walk, to learn. Parens found a striking upsurge in the aggressive drive at nine months of age—with the eruption of teeth, the destructive current of the aggressive drive increases to combat the pain.

A different kind of pain occurs when a little girl starts to receive prohibitions from her mother or others for certain acts, such as taking a doll from another child or touching a hot stove. The first prohibition has to do with selfishness, for she has to learn to share, the second with injuring herself, for she has to learn to avoid danger to her body. But at first the little girl knows only the pain of the "no."

The mother has to set limits and thus becomes the obstacle to the child's gratification of all desires. Thus hostile destructiveness is mobilized first against the mother. This conflict may take on the character of a battle of wills. In some instances there will even be screams of fury on the part of both mother and child, or slaps by the mother on the child's face or rear end.

Melanie Klein, famous British psychoanalyst, theorized that between nine to sixteen months of age, fights between a child and his mother led to the emergence of an important and lasting psychic conflict in the child. The mother causes pain at times but she is the only source of comfort to the child. This means at one moment the child feels like destroying her, the next, realizes how much he depends on her, needs her love and approval. The child has to learn to mediate between his rage and his wish to keep his mother's affection by accepting her dictates, painful though they may be.

Klein views the infant in the very early stages, before five months, as "governed by . . . aggressive tendencies against its mother's body. . . . The idea of an infant from six to twelve months trying to destroy its mother by every method at the disposal of its sadistic tendencies—with its teeth, nails and excreta and with the whole of its body—presents a horrifying not to say an unbelievable, picture to our minds."

There has been criticism of Klein's theory about the destructive intent of the infant. Of particular importance is her observation of the early relationship of the child to its parents, the result of this relationship in the child's life and later expression in his adult attitudes and behavior. She points out children add their own perceptions to these early experiences. For instance, to the mother's acts and attitudes is added the little girl's projection of her aggressive impulses and the fantasies woven around them.

Many psychoanalysts have shown that defective relationships of both women and men can be attributed to early frequent frustrations of the child by parents. A child unable to get satisfaction from one parent may turn to the other for gratification. If the child then finds he is also treated harshly by the second parent, he will be unable to develop a trusting relationship with anyone in later life. The negative experiences are taken in psychologically ("internalized"). The "bad" images of both parents (images both real and fantasied) are transferred to those in the external world. They then become targets of the original hatred and rage toward familial figures.

This is dramatically shown in the case of Joseph Kallinger described in *The Shoemaker* by Flora Rheta Schreiber. As a child and boy he was brutalized by both his adoptive parents, his hands burned, castration threatened. As an adult, he had fantasies that God was telling him to kill everyone in the world and save "mankind" (himself from his cruel adoptive mother and father).

If a little girl experiences what Dr. D. W. Winnicott, British psychoanalyst, called a "good enough" mother, one who does not excessively frustrate her, she will experience the world as "good enough." We have to take into consideration that no parent can be so perfect he never frustrates a child. The order, "You cannot have another ice cream cone, you might get an upset stomach," to a child brings forth immediate hostility. Every child wants what he wants at the moment he wants it, whether it is good for him or not.

Winnicott maintained that regardless of whether a baby is a boy or girl, the mother will "hate" her infant in at least twenty ways. In "Hate in the Countertransference" (appearing in the *International Journal of Psycho-Analysis*, 1949, Volume XXX) he explains: "I suggest that the mother hates the baby before the baby hates the mother, and before the baby can know his mother hates him." Among the reasons for the hate of a mother Winnicott mentions the interference with her private life, the danger to her body in pregnancy and at birth, and the baby's treatment of her as "an unpaid servant."

A mother "has to be able to tolerate hating her baby without doing anything about it," Winnicott writes. "She cannot express it to him. If, for fear of what she may do, she cannot hate appropriately, when hurt by her child, she must fall back on masochism and I think it is this that gives rise to the false theory of a natural masochism in women. The most remarkable thing about a mother is her ability to be hurt so much by her baby and to hate so much without paying the child out, and her ability to wait for rewards that may or may not come at a later date."

He claims the mother is helped, perhaps, by some of the nursery rhymes she sings, "which her baby enjoys but fortunately does not understand." He quotes:

> Rock-a-bye Baby, on the tree top,
> When the wind blows the cradle will rock,
> When the bough breaks the cradle will fall,
> Down will come baby, cradle and all.

Winnicott explains: "I think of a mother (a father) playing with a small infant; the infant enjoying the play and not knowing that the parent is expressing hate in the words, perhaps in birth symbolism. This is not a sentimental rhyme. Sentimentality is useless for parents, as it contains a denial of hate, and sentimentality in a mother is no good at all from the infant's point of view."

One might also say that a child, in order to acknowledge his own hate and aggression, which he will naturally feel at times, must sense that his parents are able to tolerate and accept their moments of hate without projecting them on him. The denial of all hate by a supersweet parent will only cause the child to repress his hate, feel guilty, then depressed, instead of coming to terms with it.

Thus not all psychoanalysts agree with Freud that aggression is an instinct that acts in behalf of our self-preservation. Parens does not believe it is an instinct, nor does Dr. Ives Hendrick, author of *The Facts and Theories of Psychoanalysis*. In his book he states, "All evidence of a destructive impulse in an adult can be shown to be a reaction to a thwarting of a love-impulse."

In other words, the angry reaction of the child to his mother's negative reaction to his wish for love may cause his earliest rage. The "love
impulse" appears first in the infant and if he feels rejected or abandoned
in any way by his mother, he becomes furious at her, wishes to kill
her—an angry feeling automatically carrying with it the wish the person who has caused the anger will die, as Freud said. If a mother physically abuses the child, this adds bodily insult to psychic injury and his
hate may be fanned to an intolerable fury.

If a child feels endangered by angry, cruel parents, who seem like
gods, the child fears for his very life. His desire to save it will be
stronger than his sexual desire, or influence his sexual desire in angry
ways. We may guess this occurred in the early life of Theodore Bundy,
the serial killer, who before he was electrocuted in Florida for the murder of three women in that state, confessed he had killed a number of
women amounting to "three digits," which would place it at over one
hundred. He literally in some cases "slaughtered" them, then indulged
in the sexual act.

The psychic aura in which a child is brought up and its effect on the
child's later feelings was dramatically portrayed by Margaret Mead in
her book *Sex and Temperament in Three Primitive Societies*. She describes
the vast differences between the Arapesh, a placid, nonviolent people
of New Guinea, and their neighbors, the head-hunting, cannibalistic
Mundugumors.

The Arapesh baby is never left alone by its mother. If it cries she
comforts it. The Arapesh children grow up to be gentle, cooperative.
On the other hand, the Mundugumors raise their children in harshness
and cruelty. When a baby cries out of hunger, it is not fed promptly
nor is it cuddled or made comfortable when in distress. Parents slap
their children violently for disobeying. These children, nurtured in
anger, grow into savage adults.

We may conclude it is how a child is brought up by his parents,
whether primarily with love and protectiveness and understanding or
primarily in hatred and an uncaring manner and little sympathy for the
child, that will determine whether he goes through life feeling a love
and trust in himself and others or possess little love and trust in himself
and others.

4 🔊 Rage and Adolescence

Adolescence prepares us for a life on our own, no longer dependent on a parent for decisions that must be made about future work, love affairs, marriage, having children.

Traditionally it has been assumed that adolescence is a time of revolt, rebellion and rage, usually toward parents but also often toward society. We have seen a startling rise in the adolescent use of alcohol, drugs, promiscuity and pregnancy in girls, as well as suicide.

Is such aberrant behavior natural at this stage of psychosexual development? Does adolescence *have* to be so tumultuous for both child and parent?

Research by child psychoanalysts shows adolescence does not necessarily have to be a time of emotional turmoil. Not all adolescents resort to rebellious and self-destructive behavior. If the earlier years of life have been fairly peaceful, if the adolescent feels secure in the love of his mother and father, and thus within his own life, adolescence does not have to be dramatically destructive.

If a boy or girl early in life, at the age of eighteen months and continuing throughout his or her development, has been able gradually to separate emotionally from the mother, not to be bound to her in rage and violent fantasies, he or she will not find adolescence too difficult a time as each faces permanent separation, and life with strangers.

Some psychoanalysts believe the girl's fight may be harder than the boy's because to become a separate self a girl has to transfer her love from a woman to a man, whereas a boy's object of love remains the same gender.

In her book *Adolescence: The Farewell to Childhood*, Louise J. Kaplan, PhD, points out, "The struggle, a result of personal, unique, inner conflicts is always exacerbated by the subtle social message that girls are better off if they remain childlike."

During adolescence, the incest taboo must finally be faced by both sexes, "a slow, painful process," she says. "The orders of reality cannot be carried out all at once. Bit by bit, at a great expense of emotional energy, every single one of the memories and expectations that had bound the libido to the parents must be brought up, reexperienced and reinterpreted."

She calls "this arduous piece of emotional work" the prototype for

49

mourning the death of a loved one. The adolescent, through this special version of giving up the past, accepts for the first time "the *irreversible* nature of loss" and acquires the capacity to mourn.

Similar to the mourner who will divert all the former rage he may have felt at times away from the memory of the lost one, the adolescent now "idealizes the lost past and directs the aggression elsewhere," usually toward parents and other family members, Kaplan explains. Parents can be "demoralized by the outbursts of hostility and devaluation directed at them," but though they feel bewildered and hurt most of them "try to soften for the adolescent the inevitable disappointments and despair."

Because young adolescent boys fear passivity of any kind, they are apt to act more aggressively than girls, Kaplan reports. On the other hand, a girl must come to terms with her femininity and "because of her still-lingering temptations to cling to Mother and to be cuddled and caressed—temptations that are considered 'feminine' and therefore socially acceptable—a fourteen-year-old girl might be inclined to take surprising flight from Mother."

Such flight might result in a dash toward sexual promiscuity, though "sexual intercourse for her has less to do with penises and vaginas than with reinstating a nursing situation," Kaplan states. She mentions also types of female delinquency such as shoplifting, lying, spreading false rumors "and similar 'secret' crimes that symbolize her compromise between getting the maternal love she longs for and her resentment for not getting it."

While the young adolescent boy is ashamed by any sign of femininity in his body, some young adolescent girls will do everything they can to accentuate their masculinity, acting brazenly tomboyish, as though to avoid their move into womanhood. As if asking themselves, "Am I a boy or a girl?" Kaplan points out. A girl may use obscene words, as boys do, copy their "strutting walk, Apache hairstyles and silver-studded, leather jackets." But this transitory masculine protest gives way, in most instances, to the power of the natural feminine sexual feelings.

To a lesser or greater degree, Kaplan maintains, adolescence starts with "a breakdown of controls, an eruption of unruly passions and desires, a dissolution of the civilizing trends of childhood." She adds, "But adolescence is also a narrative on the unifying tendencies of eros. We learn from adolescence that new ways of thinking, feeling, imagining, cannot be acquired overnight, fully formed. The adolescent does not relinquish the past without a struggle, without grief, without anxiety."

She describes the purpose of adolescence as not to obliterate the past but "to revise the past." In this revision, as the past is reconciled with the future, "the moral life achieves a force and prominence that rescues narcissism from isolated self-interest and aggression from mere destruction." She sees adolescence as leading to "new family units, to communities, to the species, to nature, to the cosmos." She sums up: "Given half a chance, the revolution at issue in adolescence becomes a revolution of transformation, not of annihilation."

For the girl, the issue of relinquishing dependency on the mother appears to be a main one during adolescence. But, as Judith Viorst points out in *Necessary Losses*, we also need to remember that "dependence isn't always a dirty word." She says that female dependence appears less a wish to be protected than a wish to be "part of a web of human relationships, a wish not only to get—but to give—loving care."

To need other people to help and console, "to share the good times and bad, to say 'I understand,' to be on your side—*and also to need the reverse, to need to be needed*—may lie at the heart of women's very identity," Viorst adds. She calls this "mature dependence," which means that identity for women has more to do with intimacy than separateness.

Quoting Freud's statement that "we are never so defenseless against suffering as when we love, never so helplessly unhappy as when we have lost our loved object or its love," Viorst comments that women are more apt than men to succumb to depression when love relationships end. She adds, "The logic thus seems to be that women's dependence on intimacy makes them, if not the weaker sex, the more vulnerable one."

Yet here again it seems a matter of the degree of vulnerability. If a girl has seen in her home a loving relationship between her mother and father, as an adolescent she is likely to select wisely when it comes to her choice of someone to love. She will seek the kind of man who wishes to remain true to her, who will not leave her, who wants to raise a family with her.

There are, unfortunately, many female adolescents who harm themselves in many ways, including fatally. Dr. Carol Nadelson, the first woman president of the American Psychiatric Association, who has written about adolescence, points out that in the twenty-year period between 1960 and 1980, deaths of sixteen- and seventeen-year-olds in vehicular accidents increased more than 40 percent, homicides over 230 percent. These are dramatic increases and tell us much about the hopeless feelings that can destroy many adolescents.

Drug use among twelve- to seventeen-year-old whites increased in this twenty-year period by almost 140 percent and the use of alcohol by 56 percent. The delinquency rate of ten- to seventeen-year-olds rose by over 130 percent. Suicide increased by 140 percent.

Dr. Nadelson says, "The issue that has been most compelling and has caused the greatest concern is the tragedy of teenage suicide." This is the second leading cause of death in adolescents, following closely behind accidents, many of which can be seen as equivalent to suicide, caused by the wish to destroy the self and/or others.

It is estimated that about twenty-five thousand suicides take place in this country each year, and approximately ten times as many suicide attempts are made. Five thousand of these suicides, or one-fifth, are adolescents and 12 percent of suicide attempts are made by adolescents; 10 percent of those who attempt suicide later succeed.

Most attempts are made by girls but the ratio of completed suicides is three to two, male to female, though this statistic appears to be changing as an increasing number of teenage girls commit suicide. Suicide also appears related to age, accounting for 2.4 percent of all deaths in the first half of adolescence and 8 percent in the second half.

Declaring this society has not been alone in concern for adolescents, Dr. Nadelson quotes Aristotle as saying, "The young are in character prone to desire and ready to carry any desire they may have formed into action. . . . They are changeful, too, and fickle in their desires, which are as transitory as they are vehement; for their wishes are keen without being permanent, like a sick man's fit of hunger and thirst. They are passionate, irascible, apt to be carried away by their impulses. . . . They carry everything too far, whether it be love or hatred or anything else."

She also referred to Shakespeare's words in *The Winter's Tale*: "I would there were no age between sixteen and three-and-twenty, or that youth would sleep out the rest; for there is nothing in the between but getting wenches with child, wronging the ancientry, stealing, fighting."

She concludes, "As Shakespeare reminded us, we cannot close our eyes, but we both—parents and children—must tolerate the anxiety and uncertainty adolescents experience. There is no turning back."

She adds, "We often fail to remember that a new parental identity must also emerge as parents return to their childless days and take on a new role in society. At times, parental reactions parallel those of their children, and the adolescent may lose the reassurance and support of parental authority and stability. In this process, parents, society and adolescents are often pitted against each other in a struggle toward mutual definition, tolerance and responsibility."

Our newspapers, magazines, movies and television screens abound in accounts of suicide by teenage girls and boys. Often the suicide occurs after a love affair ends and the rejected one feels an abandonment he cannot bear by "the one and only."

To understand why an adolescent (or anyone) chooses to end his life rather than live it out, we have to recognize that suicide is the wish to murder turned on the self. The adolescent girl or boy who commits suicide is in fantasy killing a mother and/or father who in some way has hurt them.

First there is the impulse to kill—definitely a hostile, destructive one—which is turned on the self as the adolescent thinks, "Because I wish too intensely to kill, I must destroy myself." The suicidal person punishes himself in the same fashion he wished to punish his parents.

The self-flagellation, the masochism, that leads to suicide starts early in childhood with the wish to gain revenge on the mother or father who has, usually in many ways, angered and frustrated the natural emotional development of the child, either by neglect or violence or sexual abuse. The child is finally overcome by a depression he cannot conquer.

The adolescent who kills himself is showing his rage at his parent. What may appear like an "immediate" tragedy has roots in far earlier life. When a girl of fifteen or sixteen takes her own life she is telling her parents, "You didn't love me enough. My anger at you is so great I wanted to destroy you. But instead I kill myself and I hope you suffer the guilt." Notes left by suicide victims attest to the wish that those they love will in some way feel despair and responsibility for the death.

There is also the slow suicide of today—the taking of drugs, consumption of too much alcohol and driving recklessly on the nation's highways. Suicide statistics show that at least seven thousand adolescents a year kill themselves in these ways while an estimated half a million make attempts but are saved.

In their choice of the way of suicide, male and female adolescents act differently. Men tend to be more violent—they hang themselves, shoot themselves, throw their bodies off rooftops or high bridges. Women select more passive means of suicide—sleeping pills, drowning or gas.

Adolescent girls who are victims of early incest often commit suicide: either slowly through drugs or alcohol, or acting out of impulse. An-

other form of self-destructive behavior is to become a prostitute—
studies show that a majority of prostitutes have been sexually abused as
girls by their fathers. A recent survey of the Chicago Vice Commission
found that 51 out of 103 women prostitutes reported having their first
sexual experience with their fathers.

A sixteen-year-old prostitute was considering suicide when she decided instead to go to a mental health clinic. She revealed that her
older sister, also a prostitute, had committed suicide by taking an over-
dose of drugs the month before. She confessed that both she and her
sister had been sexually abused since they were three years old by their
father.

A mother is the role model for her daughter in many ways, and one
of her most important behavior patterns is the way she feels and acts
about her own aggression. Thus we may ask, Does a mother express her
aggression in a hostile manner or constructive assertiveness?

If, for various reasons, a mother has not wanted her daughter—she
interferes with the mother's freedom, her mother wanted a boy, the
mother is no longer in love with her husband, the little girl halts the
mother's career—the mother's resentment will be apparent in the way
she feels toward her daughter all through childhood and adolescence.

A twenty-three-year-old librarian told her closest friend, "I was
aware when I was a little girl that my mother resented me. She would
tell me over and over that if I hadn't been born she could have studied
to become a famous opera star."

This was fantasy on the part of the mother, rationalization of her inability to build a career. Even with a daughter, or several children, she
could have studied singing. Many successful women performers have
raised children and had enjoyable careers. This mother was blaming her
daughter unfairly for depriving her of the limelight. A mother who used
her aggression assertively would have worked at whatever she wished
and also brought up her daughter.

If a mother has a sarcastic, biting manner, the daughter will generally
copy this. A mother's attitude toward life, either optimistic or pessimis-
tic, will be emotionally absorbed by the daughter. After all, who else
is there for her to emulate in the feminine role but the one who is nearest and dearest?

A mother is apt to hate in a daughter any characteristic the mother
hates in herself. The daughter may mirror a selfishness she copied from
her mother, which the mother cannot tolerate. Or a daughter will be

careless about keeping her room clean or her appearance neat and this will anger the mother, who has the same tendencies.

One daughter of sixteen, whose mother reproached her for leaving the house with dresses that were not ironed or had hems torn, said in surprise, "But I've seen you wear unironed dresses and hanging hems." The mother laughed, realized her daughter copied her, and said, "I guess we both hate to iron and sew."

An adolescent daughter may dislike a mother because of her hostile manner but daughters may also be unreasonably hostile toward a mother because oedipal rivalry has not been resolved. Especially in this day when the divorce rate is high and many fathers have left the home, daughters will blame their mother for the father's absence.

An eighteen-year-old college sophomore told a classmate, also the victim of a broken home, "I can't forgive my mother for acting so insensitively that she drove my father out of the house. She criticized him unmercifully all the time. No wonder he found another wife."

Her classmate said, "My mother also made my father's life a real hell. Then told him to leave. Can you believe *that?*"

Neither daughter, because of a deep oedipal attachment, could look at her mother with unbiased eyes. It always takes two to break up a marriage. Blaming one or the other parent means the one who blames does not understand that both were unable to maintain a warm, loving relationship.

When a daughter is too dependent on a mother, cannot leave home to live on her own at an age when it is appropriate to do so, the mother usually has for years maintained a selfish, hostile attachment to the daughter. A number of young women spend years of their lives, if not their entire lives, living with a lone mother, keeping her company, usually supporting her. Such a daughter holds back a buried rage, unable to break free and live on her own.

The mother who is assertive rather than hostilely aggressive knows it is part of her maternal job to allow her daughter to become gradually independent, gain a sense of her own self. Such a mother does not use the daughter to fulfill her own needs but helps her to achieve one of the most difficult tasks in life—to give up the fantasies of childhood that keep her infantilized in an emotional sense.

A twenty-one-year-old daughter had lived all her life in Tarrytown, New York, twenty miles north of New York City, commuting during her college days at Barnard. She was an only child and her father had left the house four years before to marry another woman. Neither mother nor daughter had spoken about the daughter's plans after graduation.

The daughter faced her mother when she had graduated, said quietly, "Mother, I'm moving away to live in New York."

Tears formed in the mother's eyes. She said accusingly, "Why are you doing this to me?"

"I'm not doing anything to you, mother," she said. "I have a job in the city as an editor at a small publishing house."

"You should commute, like you've done during college," the mother protested. "It's only a forty-minute train ride."

"I'm sorry, mother," she said. "It wasn't an easy decision. But I think it's time I left the nest."

"What'll I do?" wailed the mother. "You're my whole life."

"That's just the trouble," the daughter said. "It's not healthy for us to live together. We should give each other space. We can get together whenever we want."

The mother burst into tears but the daughter was strong enough not to give in. She realized she would be sacrificing the rest of her life if she remained in the same house as her mother, much as she loved her. Within three years the daughter was married and the mother had re-married a widower who lived five houses away. If the daughter had remained at home in all probability each would not have felt free to consider a marital partner.

This daughter's ability to be assertive, rather than to give in to her mother's dependent attitude, which the daughter sensed would cripple her emotionally, freed them both to act more maturely. While at college, the daughter had realized the importance of breaking free of a parent as she had seen many of her classmates do.

A problem that has attracted wide attention is teenage pregnancy, which often stems from rage at parents. This country has the highest rate among western nations, a rate that has steadily moved up in the last two decades. It is estimated that more than half the population of fifteen- to nineteen-year-olds in the United States and a fifth of the thirteen- to fourteen-year-olds are sexually active and the young woman runs the risk of pregnancy.

Of the more than ten million adolescent women age fifteen to nineteen, one in ten becomes pregnant, almost two million each year. In New York City public schools there were thirty-five thousand pregnancies in 1986 reported by the Board of Education. This led to the opening of health clinics in the public schools where contraceptives could be obtained. At first they were available to any teenager, then, under protest from parents, within several weeks they were limited to eighteen-year-old women.

The rate in 1982 was 185 pregnancies per 1,000 black fifteen- to nineteen-year-olds and 96 per 1,000 for white girls of this age range. Of the total pregnancies, almost 30 percent had live births and more than 20 percent that were reported had abortions. For those fourteen and under, there were almost 30,000 pregnancies, half of which ended in abortion and one-third in live births.

It has been reported that 88 percent of teenagers are sexually active before seeking contraceptives. Those communities that have lowered their pregnancy rates offer active educational programs and provide access to contraception. Successful programs generally advise sexually active teenagers how to obtain and use contraceptives, how to find prenatal care and how to get back into school. One school installed a day care center as a "grim reminder" to other students that "parenthood is no picnic."

Adolescent passion occurs in all kinds of families—the rich and the poor, the white and the black, the intellectual and the illiterate or semiliterate. Families who raise children with love and care undoubtedly have a far lower rate of adolescent pregnancy than those whose children are neglected or given little love. The latter often will indulge in sex, hoping to find a relationship that will allow them to leave home for a better life. This is true for both boys and girls.

That the relationships seldom prove permanent, that babies are born out of wedlock, is the result of wishes that could not possibly come true. It takes a certain amount of maturity to ensure a lasting relationship at any age and particularly during adolescence.

But at least this country has come a long way from the days when Nathaniel Hawthorne wrote *The Scarlet Letter,* in which Hester Prynne had to wear the letter "A" for *adulteress* across the top of her dress. She was made to show her shame before the Massachusetts community for having a child out of wedlock.

The illegitimate child is no longer considered an outcast, nor is his mother. Emphasis is not on her "shame" now but on trying to educate adolescents, to bring them the knowledge that a child needs two parents in order to have a successful emotional life and to reach what we call "maturity" with a fair chance of living peacefully and happily with a mother and father he loves.

5 🕎 Rage in Women

"**I**t's a dirty trick blaming Eve for our fall from grace," one man says to another in the British film *Last Bus to Woodstock*, a television murder mystery featuring Inspector Morse, appearing in New York on Channel 31, January 26, 1989.

Ever since Eve women have been blamed for mankind's ejection from the Garden of Eden into the cruel, cold world of reality. Because a woman supposedly could not resist the gift of an apple from a snake (was the snake masculine or feminine?) man believes he was thrown out of Paradise to suffer over the centuries. The story of Adam and Eve's fall from grace was invented of course by a man. A woman, at this time in history, would not have been permitted to take part in the writing of the Bible.

Far more than men, women have suffered historically, have been thought of as the "evil one." Joan of Arc was burned at the stake, as were the "witches" of medieval days. Women have been forced to deny their undoubtedly at times flaming rage, humble themselves before men, accept whatever violence or calumny man has wanted to inflict on them.

Even unto the present day. A headline on the editorial page of *The New York Times* on January 30, 1989, read: "India's Dowry Murders Mark Rise in Violence against Women." Hanna Papanek of Boston wrote *The Times* on January 19 a letter describing this violence. She is a senior research associate in Boston University's Center for Asian Development Studies.

She started off praising the newspaper's "spirited reporting" on January 15 of "the dreadful dowry murders of some Hindu wives in India, 'where a husband kills a wife for failing to deliver on a request material goods from her father as a continuing dowry payment.'"

She called these murders "a modern phenomenon, not to be confused with the largely extinct custom of sati, in which some groups forced widows to commit suicide on their husbands' cremation pyres." She explained that the "dowry" murders are different, are "part of a vicious competition for status and luxury consumer goods by urban middle-class families greedily seeking wealth at the expense of their

58

daughters." Newly married daughters are sometimes virtual hostages against the payments promised by parents to their in-laws, whose demands sometimes escalate after the marriage. It is then husbands threaten to kill their wives—actually do if parents fail to come across with payments.

Both families share complicity in the murders, Ms. Papanek says. The young women despair not only because their in-laws, with whom they often live, make threats of death but also because they are neglected by their own parents when they complain of the harassment. Ms. Papanek cites "the wider context of violence against women," claiming "these harassments are part of a greater worldwide trend of increased violence against women—a trend United States readers see illustrated daily or weekly in reports on battered women."

Violence against women is reported in Arab countries, in Brazil and other parts of South America and the world where women lack equal rights. South Africa is noted for its mistreatment of women, including young girls, as incest is practiced freely.

In our country we take pride in the fact that women are slowly achieving equal rights after a fight that started at the turn of the century with the suffrage movement. Yet one of the most difficult tasks for women in this so-called age of liberation is to accept fully—to feel and to acknowledge—their right to rage when they are exploited by men, physically, economically or emotionally.

Women have been denied this right so long that acceptance seems alien; they believe they must suffer in silence. Their ability to feel anger, then decide whether it is justified, or rage at a fantasied wrong, appears more difficult for women than acceptance of the liberation of sexual desires. The aggressive impulse is believed the most devastating to admit.

A thirty-year-old actress appearing on Broadway told her psychoanalyst after a year on the couch that she was finally able to say she was "furious" because he took notes as she spoke and she could hear his pen scratching the paper. She admitted, "For a year I have not been able to tell you of my fury. Yet I could speak freely almost from the first session of the many affairs I had and how I felt like a prostitute who went unpaid."

Thus the sexual desires of women are more consciously acknowledged with ease in fantasies of love and eroticism but the wishes and fantasies emerging from hostile aggression remain buried. No doubt this has occurred because throughout the centuries woman has had to deny her rage more than her sensuality in order to exist in comparative safety with a man.

Studies show that many wives even feel sorry for husbands who beat them, even though these women live in constant terror of the next beating. A few may finally resort to violence—as in the film, *The Burning Bed,* in which the wife sets fire to the house—but the majority are passive, endure their physical pain and emotional despair. They continue to live in an atmosphere of hopelessness, helplessness and despair, somehow feeling they deserve the abuse, are powerless to change their lives.

Studies of battered women show that brutality was common in their childhood—either they were beaten by their father or mother or they daily witnessed their father assaulting other members of the family, including the mother.

Battered wives remain with cruel husbands for one strong, unconscious reason seldom faced by the woman—the husband is expressing the wife's own wish for revenge that she has never been able either to admit or act out. She gets vicarious delight from identifying with the cruel husband even though the blows are inflicted on her.

Women are supposed to be the nurturers within the family, understand all anger that emanates from husband and child, smile sweetly, never lose their tempers. But many women are unable to do this as the headlines in New York City newspapers and other cities attest. Some kill their babies, unable to stand their crying or the incessant changing of diapers (the woman's own mother communicated distaste to her as a child for such tasks).

We are just starting to understand how many young women are unprepared to be "good mothers." They marry to flee unhappy homes, ill-equipped emotionally to raise a child, as are the male partners they pick for an overnight sexual fling or a few months of supposed closeness.

In her eloquent exploration of women's anger, Harriet Goldhor Lerner, psychologist at The Menninger Foundation, describes women as having been taught to hold rage within. . . . "The taboos against our feeling and expressing anger are so powerful that even *knowing* when we are angry is not a simple matter. When a woman shows her anger she is likely to be dismissed as irrational or worse."

She also points out that the "oversweet" woman, the "butter wouldn't melt in her mouth kind of woman," only perpetuates hurtful fantasies and feelings buried within since childhood. At a high cost to her awareness of both her conscious and unconscious anger, wishes, fears and thoughts, she goes through the years suppressing all rage.

The grim way some women look at their lives was illustrated by two lines from the movie *Cousins*. A daughter, married to a man having an affair with another woman as the daughter herself indulges in an affair with a married cousin, says to her mother, "I haven't been happy in a long time."

Her mother retorts bitterly, "Who says life is supposed to be happy?"

But on the optimistic side, in recent years new freedoms for women have taken place. They appear in every area from religion to basketball and baseball and they are increasing all the time. For instance, in Boston on February 11, 1989, the Reverend Barbara Clementine Harris, a fifty-five-year-old priest, became the first woman consecrated as a bishop in the Episcopal Church.

Even so, at the ceremony, a representative of the church's strongly conservative Prayer Book Society walked to a microphone and called the consecration of a woman as bishop "a sacrilegious imposture." The audience jeered and booed as Bishop Edmond L. Browning, the presiding bishop of the church, begged for silence, and the ceremony proceeded.

In other areas of life no such objections were made when a woman entered the work arena for the first time. In spite of their fear of being labeled "hostilely aggressive," a growing number of women have placed their constructive energy into furthering their careers in government, the law, science, sports and academic achievements.

A few have dared break through the ironclad barrier against entering a sacrosanct field supposedly "for men only," as Bishop Barbara Harris did. Dr. Jeane J. Kirkpatrick, former Ambassador to Italy and professor of international law at Columbia University, became the first woman to serve as United States Permanent Representative to the United Nations. As President Reagan's chief delegate, she served four years until mid-1985.

When Dr. Kirkpatrick addressed the Women's Forum on December 19, 1984, in New York City, she expressed mild rage at men. She said she had been called "tough" and "confrontational" by male reporters and added, "It was a while before I noticed that *none* of my male colleagues, who often delivered more 'confrontational' speeches than I, were labeled as 'confrontational.' I have concluded that it is extremely *unlikely* that *any* woman who arrives at a very high level in any public activity is confrontational. If women were, they would have long since been eliminated."

She minced no words as she told the Women's Forum, "What do I want to say about it all, finally? I want to say that I think that sexism is alive. It's alive in the United Nations, in the Secretariat. It's alive in the United States government. It's alive in American politics. I've seen enough of Democratic politics at high levels to know that it's bipartisan."

She added, "And I also want to say that sexism is not unconquerable, if one can avoid getting and staying angry and wasting one's energies on rage."

She called the United Nations "a heavily male preserve." She maintained the reason that literature on women in politics and women in power has not focused specifically on international affairs, on diplomacy and on defense, "is that male preemption of these fields is so ubiquitous, so 'normal,' so taken for granted that it is virtually invisible, *even* to most women accustomed to thinking unthinkable thoughts about sex roles."

Throughout the nation, however, there has been a steadily growing number of women candidates for national and state offices, very important to the political progress of women. The first woman in Congress was Jeanette Rankin of Montana who, in 1914, became that state's leading suffragist and was elected to the House of Representatives two years later. Miss Rankin, a pacifist, became the only one to vote against the United States' entry into both World Wars.

Women are gradually entering the world of science, inhabited only by men until 1903. That year Madame Marie Sklodowska Curie became the first woman to win the Nobel Prize in Physics, sharing it with her husband, Dr. Pierre Curie, for the discovery of radium and polonium. Maria Mitchell of Nantucket won honors in the world of astronomy.

In literature, Nobel Prizes have gone to Selma Lagerlöf, Grazia Deledda, Sigrid Undset, Pearl Buck and Gabriela Mistral. A number of women writers have increasingly contributed to the literature of the world. No longer does a Baronne Dudevant, born Amandine Aurora Lucie Dupin in 1803, have to write under the name George Sand.

Women's climb to fame has been slow in man's world of painting. Mary Cassatt, Rosa Bonheur and Vivien-Lapage achieved honors in Europe. The first prominent woman artist in America was Georgia

O'Keefe, who died recently at the age of ninety-eight, a key figure in the art of the twentieth century.

Women in greater numbers are entering the profession of law as well as other areas. Jean Hails became the first woman president of the Associated Builders and Contractors, leader of the eighteen thousand members of the national association of construction companies. Nancy Lopez, mother of two children and wife of the Mets' third baseman, Ray Knight (in 1988), has won many national golf tournaments, hitting a golf ball as far as most men do. Nancy Lieberman was the first woman to achieve fame in basketball as a member of the Dallas Diamonds. Perry Lee Barber became the first woman chosen as an umpire for major league spring training games—a step toward being accepted into the big league official games.

More women have entered the field of medicine. Between 1954 and 1984 the proportion of women in American medical schools rose from 4.7 percent to 32.6 percent. Women in greater numbers are becoming psychologists, psychiatrists and psychoanalysts. The first woman on the Board of Trustees of the American Medical Association was Louise Gloeckner, MD who served as vice president and a member of the Board in 1969-70.

A strong barrier against women healers of the mind was broken when Dr. Carol Nadelson became the first woman president of the American Psychiatric Association in its 140 years of history. In her presidential address at the annual meeting of the Association in May 1986, addressing psychiatrists from all over the world, she said that in her election the Association "had moved beyond connecting gender and leadership," and hoped this "reflected a more general societal direction."

She concluded that "supporting female leadership is a process that will take time because it can't be tokenism but must represent fundamental change. In the past women have not felt welcome or encouraged."

It is interesting that women were the ones who originally sought the help of Freud—depressed, sometimes delusional women, hiding intense rage at how they were treated by men and the parents of childhood. Through their unhappy childhood revelations on the couch, they contributed to the early development of Freud's theories. He paid special tribute to Bertha Pappenheim, known as "Anna O.," for leading him to psychoanalysis when she described the help she received from Dr. Josef Breuer, Freud's mentor, as "the talking cure."

Her buried rage had caused her to become physically paralyzed and to speak in "gibberish," as the schizophrenic often does. Breuer listened to her, helped her gain the psychic strength to talk sanely of what troubled her, and she recovered her sanity.

Today a growing number of unhappy and depressed women seek analysts so they may know and express their hidden rage. One woman, forty years old, a literary agent, told her psychoanalyst as she ended four years of therapy, "Thank you for helping me face my inner anger. Butter wouldn't melt in my mouth when I first came here. I know you have worked very hard to get me to admit I might be very angry at times."

She went on, "I now realize how I repressed my fury at my mother and father over the years as I grew up. I'm getting more familiar with my anger, some of it justified, some unjustified. I no longer blame my parents for what happened to me. I expected too much of them and they expected too much of me."

She sighed, confessed, "I know too why I never married. I didn't trust a man to stay with me, I was filled with such torment. I thought my precious career was the only thing that mattered. I didn't need anybody on whom to depend, I'd show the world I could go it alone."

As she faced her hidden anger for the first time in her life and realized neither she nor a man with whom she might become involved had to be "perfect," she could think of a relationship as "sharing" and "trustworthy." A fifty-year-old writer, recently divorced, asked her to represent him on the sale to publishers of his mystery books and they fell in love, married.

When women can face their rage—both at the past and at the current inequities in society—they lose the guilt that shadows rage. They free more of their assertive energy, an energy that is not tinged with wishes for revenge. They have learned they are entitled to anger when taken advantage of—they now know the difference between hostility founded in hate and the feeling of assertiveness that leads to productive activity.

Many a psychoanalyst has said to a woman patient, "You don't have to be an angel, giving in to everyone. You must know when you are in the right and speak up. Not angrily but with conviction. Don't be scared of the other person as though he were the punitive parent of your childhood."

A number of women bury their rage at friends who constantly attack them verbally without cause. A forty-five-year-old fashion executive had been friends since high school with a woman who always tore her down out of jealousy. This critical woman, though she had wanted a career as an artist, remained a housewife and lived in the suburbs with her husband and three children.

One day the fashion executive decided she was not going to tolerate the criticism any longer. Her friend, over tea at the Plaza, criticized her latest designs for women's dresses, saying, "There's nothing original about them."

The fashion executive looked her friend of long standing in the eyes, said, "What makes you qualified to judge them? When will you stop attacking everything I do because you are so jealous?"

The friend erupted in anger. She said viciously, "Who in hell do you think you are? Gloria Vanderbilt?"

"I have no illusions about my work," the fashion executive said quietly. "I accept myself for what I can do. But I will not accept your constant condemnation of my hard work."

The friend stood up, flung a twenty-dollar bill on the marble table, said, "This will take care of my part of the meal," and stormed out. She did not call to apologize nor did the fashion executive. The latter felt sad: she may have lost a long-time friend but she had gained a new self-esteem because at long last she had decided not to accept these vindictive attacks.

Realizing her anger was justified, she felt no need to respond to her friend's rage with anger, but could use reason. She knew if she continued taking insults she would only demean herself further. She had decided she was going to stand up for herself and that day had offered the crucial moment.

While rage is often met with rage, a woman who has made the conscious decision not to tolerate pain inflicted emotionally by another often finds she need not erupt in anger, but can composedly explain the way she feels exploited and announce she is accepting the exploitation no longer. Much of the time the exploiter will react as the woman above did and the woman who has been exploited must be prepared to have additional anger hurled at her head. But she is now willing to stand up for herself, no matter the cost.

Actual violence is not as widespread as fantasies of violence. There is an old saying, "Sticks and stones may break my bones but words will never hurt me," yet words are used in anger and do hurt in an emotional way. A common method of expressing rage is through the use of "dirty" words—words related to excretory functions or sexual activity, like "shit" and "fuck." They show contempt and hostility but also the close connection between sexual and aggressive fantasies.

The major obscene word in our language is not "fuck" but a word far more meaningful in our early life, according to Dr. Leo Stone, noted psychoanalyst. Tracing the history of the word "fuck" and its appearance in literature and dictionaries, he concludes that the word "suck" is more obscene.

He points out the similarity "unconscious rhyme relation" of the "heretofore taboo word 'fuck' and the word 'suck.' He suggests that the "pleasure and often guilty excitement" that accompany the use of the word "fuck," are displaced onto it from the earlier, far more tabooed process of "sucking," associated unconsciously with the mother who once was "sucked." He comments, "This would not be too surprising, insofar as it is sucking and suckling that distinguish the entire vertebrate class to which we belong."

Dreams offer us a route to the understanding of the rage and violence in us we have repressed because of childhood experiences or distortions of those experiences at a time we did not as yet possess much ability to use reason. If we understand a dream we can bring past and present together, become aware of conflicts that have remained unmastered and unresolved. Thus we may free ourselves from endless repetition of stereotyped, destructive behavior that may be dominating our lives.

One woman dreamed she was chased by gangsters. They caught her, locked her in a room in the attic of a deserted town house, threatened to kill her if she tried to escape. The door suddenly opened and a man resembling Charles Bronson approached, knife in hand. As he was about to plunge it into her, she woke screaming.

The woman, in remembering the dream, realized she thought of her husband, who looked like Charles Bronson, as somewhat of a gangster. They had waged an angry fight the night before as he forbade her to sign up for an evening course in the arts. He claimed it would take too much of her time away from her two small sons. She had felt furious and in the dream her fury was portrayed in reverse, as dreams often do—the killer sought her. In our dreams we play all the roles, the dream is our creation and she was both gangster and victim.

A twenty-nine-year-old mother told her therapist of a dream in which she and her seven-year-old daughter were fleeing "a drunken stranger" through what she described as "a black forest." Suddenly she stopped in her flight, turned on the stranger, grabbed him by the throat and squeezed it so violently that all the blood gushed out of his body "in a black stream," leaving only skin and bones. She woke horrified.

"How could I possibly do that to a man?" she asked the therapist. "And who was the man?"

"You refer to him as 'a drunken stranger.' Was there anything familiar about him?" asked the therapist.

"I don't think so," she said.

"What man in your life drank a lot?"

"I've told you that," she replied. "My father, of course."

"Do you remember any time your father chased you while he was drunk?"

Tears came to her eyes as she recalled, "When I was fifteen, I got all dressed up for the junior prom. I came down the stairs in my first party dress—black satin with shoulder straps of rhinestones. I felt like a princess. My father, a glass of scotch in his hand, ordered me to go upstairs and change my dress. He called it too sexy. He said I should put on my old blue taffeta. I refused. He slapped my face, ordered me to do as he said and tore at one of the rhinestone shoulder straps. I burst into tears and ran upstairs shrieking that I wasn't going to the prom."

She stopped, remembering, then went on, "My mother sewed the strap back on. She told me my father didn't mean what he said, wouldn't remember it the next morning. Then she helped me sneak out of the house through the kitchen door so he wouldn't see me. The next day he had forgotten all about it."

"But you didn't forget," said the therapist. "You have repressed your anger at the father who chased you, like the stranger did in your dream. You have wanted to kill your father, choke every bit of blood out of his body for demeaning and humiliating you that night. And probably other nights."

He added, "The black forest represented your black dress, the blackness also covers the forest, symbolic of pubic hair. Your father was punishing you for looking too sexy in the dress, accusing you of wanting to seduce men and you understood this was his real accusation. You hated him for making you feel so cheap. Depriving you of self-esteem."

"I never dared admit a moment of hatred for my father," she admitted.

"It's dangerous to defy a drunken man. He might maim or kill you in his anger. Instead, you had to repress your 'black rage.'"

The therapist then asked what she had seen or thought the day be-

fore the dream that might have stirred the memory recalled in the
dream. She thought a moment, then said in surprise, "I stood for a long
time in front of a window at Lord and Taylor's staring as though mes-
merized at a black dress with a rhinestone collar."

The therapist said, "The sight of that black dress with the rhinestones awakened memories of the earlier black dress in your life. One
that caused torment and a rage you had to deny all these years to keep
the love of your father."

The stuff of dreams protects us from knowing consciously memories
we believe dangerous to our self-esteem. But such memories, if revealed
to the light of consciousness through deciphering our dreams, can increase self-esteem. We no longer have to deny the buried rage and guilt
that have lowered our image of ourselves over the years.

One cause of rage in women that men will never experience is what
Dr. Norman Shelly, psychoanalyst, calls "the bloody rage" that con-
sumes many of them during the monthly menstrual period. He has
found in analyzing woman patients that their anger at what they believe a "burden," "a painful experience twelve times a year," or a "demeaning act beyond their control," is often a powerful one.

He points out that the fantasies of the little girl before she reaches
this monthly break in her life have much to do with her feelings about
it. If her mother has accepted the period as natural, leading eventually
to the birth of wanted babies, the girl is likely to see it as such. But
if her mother reacts to her own menstrual period as annoying, hurtful
in any way or shows anger at it, the little girl is likely to have the same
reactions.

Also, the little girl who deeply envies boys (because they have the
valued penis and because they do not suffer this monthly flow of blood)
is apt to be angrier than the little girl who has given up her natural wish
to be a boy (Freud says little children, at the start, believe they can be
both sexes).

One hurtful way man has demeaned woman through the ages, lowering her self-esteem, is by the words he originated to refer to her. In a
British book aptly titled *Man-Made Language*, Dale Spender describes
all the subtle and not so subtle ways in which through verbiage the
"masculine" is associated with the "norm" while the "feminine" is dero-
gated and demeaned by the men who coined and continued to use the
words.

For instance, words with negative connotations are applied to
women even though they are also used, without stigma, to designate

the same state or condition in men. *Spinster* and *bachelor* refer scornfully to an unmarried adult but the positive state of bachelordom is applied to a man—the "bachelor" is always greeted eagerly at a party—whereas a "spinster" is shunned, looked at with disdain when she enters a room.

Spender maintains there is a relationship between woman's devaluation in language and her devaluation in society. She cites the word "bitch" applied in derogation to women, a word used originally to designate a female dog. Referring to "sexism in language," Spender cites a study showing that there are 220 words for a sexually promiscuous female and only 20 for a sexually promiscuous male.

She comments, "This would seem to indicate that the language—as a system—embodies sexual inequality and that it is not women who enjoy the advantage." In the use of the word *tramp*, for example, there is a shift to a negative and sexual meaning when applied to females (synonym for prostitute or hooker) as opposed to males (a destitute man who must wander the streets because he has no money).

Spender points out that men, rather than women, have accumulated the economic resources of the earth, according to United Nations statistics of 1980. Males earn more than 90 percent of the world's wages and own 99 percent of the world's resources. Therefore, she says, it is the men of the earth who "are in a position to insist on the validity of their own views and values . . . indisputably in a position to be heard." Women have known for centuries that men have been "the undeservedly dominant sex, and that their dominance is reflected and reininforced in the language and by language use," she adds. By their choice of the words they use to refer to women, they "have used their power to silence women, to censor women's challenge."

Spender gives as example of further derogation the fact that when a woman achieves success she is described as being "as good as a male" but there is no expression for "as good as a female." Spender concludes: "For women who do not wish to be compared to men there is 'nowhere to go' in the language. This is one way of expressing the concept of negative semantic space for women." The expressions *lady* doctor, *female* surgeon, *woman* lawyer, show that a woman carries what Spender calls "their minus maleness" as they are "still branded as women" who enter a male sphere.

In the past women have been expected by society to appear weak and subservient, not allowed to question the authority of men. But today, as women gain more equality, one important question faces them: Will a woman, no matter how much equality she gains in the statutes and the workplace, feel the same lack of self-esteem many a man feels if she does not possess an inner sense of emotional security? Which means she has faced her aggressive and sexual conflicts and has no need to project them on her husband, children, parents, friends, colleagues.

The drive to achieve, if a compulsive one, like many men possess, may interfere with a woman's emotional security and affect her capacity to love, to share, to give of herself—if her aim is to "have a mind like a man, work like a man." She will then be victim of the same emotional insecurity many men, who have not solved their aggressive and sexual conflicts, possess.

Freud recognized the problems inherent in giving separate interpretations to the concepts of masculinity and femininity. In describing separate behaviors for man and woman he wrote in 1933:

"In the sphere of human sexual life you soon see how inadequate it is to make masculine behavior coincide with activity and feminine with passivity. . . . The further you go from the narrow sexual sphere the more obvious will the 'error of superimposition' become. Women can display great activity in various directions, men are not able to live in company with their own kind unless they develop a large amount of passive adaptability."

He added, "If you now tell me that these facts go to prove precisely that both men and women are bisexual in the psychological sense, I shall conclude that you have decided in your own minds to make 'active' coincide with 'masculine' and 'passive' with 'feminine.' But I advise you against it. It seems to me to serve no useful purpose and adds nothing to our knowledge."

Unfortunately, too many women still accept the masculine bias and outdo men in self-deprecation, colluding in the age-old subjugation of women. Because of her feelings of inferiority, a woman envies and fears man's aggressive and sexual power, submits to a man out of that fear, then feels an underlying contempt both for herself and the subjugating man who exploits her.

Woman's only measure of revenge has been this hidden contempt. In past centuries women felt enslaved, allowed only to feel contempt for the brutal master as long as they did not reveal it and incur the master's wrath. The dramatic exception were the Amazons, who openly sought to defeat and subjugate men. But most women carefully hid their wish for vengeance.

The free woman of today must have the courage to be aggressive, as Dr. Martin Grotjahn says, which means "for her to fight for the unjust, the downtrodden, and against the thoughtless men who cannot stop playing with toxic and nuclear material."

Freud wrote Marie Bonaparte, his friend and colleague, "The great question that has never been answered and which I have not yet been able to answer, despite my thirty years of research into the feminine soul, is 'What does a woman want?'"

If the woman of today is asked this, she is likely to agree she wants to be loved and to love, marry and raise children, seek a career if she wishes. Some do achieve their goals. But a number do not feel any happier or more fulfilled in spite of marriage, children and career.

Perhaps the important point is that when it comes to decisions of all kinds, a woman should feel she has made a thoughtful, wise choice rather than a driven, anxiety-ridden one. The choice should come out of her inner convictions, not out of fantasies that are unrealistic.

Women cannot blame a marriage or children or a career for making them unhappy. If they are unhappy they should face the internal conflicts causing the unhappiness. A woman may still blame society and/or men for real, ongoing injustices but not for an inner sense of confusion or inadequacy that persists despite her many external gains.

Nor can she blame "society" or "men" for her repressed anger that may have little or nothing to do with external reality but has blocked her ability to sublimate her aggression in a way that will bring her pleasure, not rage.

"So do we put our life into our every act," Emerson said. This is shown no more truly, or tragically, than in the feeling of rage that, if it is not realistic, spells out the whole of a traumatic childhood and the crippling of the aggressive spirit—now used to destroy rather than to build and enhance life.

Woman has gained equality with man in some important areas. First, there was the hard-won suffrage battle. In the past few years we have seen the first woman run for the vice presidency of the United States and the first appointment of a woman to the Supreme Court of the United States.

On the other hand there are areas in our democratic country where women are still drastically exploited. For one, they are often denied "equal justice" in the courts of this nation. This was stated in a recent report by a special New York State Task Force on Women in the Courts that studied the New York courts for two years. It was composed of state legislators, judges, professors and lawyers.

The twenty-three-member panel concluded that female lawyers were

"routinely" demeaned and treated patronizingly by male judges and at-
torneys. The credibility of female witnesses was sometimes questioned
because some judges viewed women as "emotional" and "untrustwor-
thy." Other judges did not recognize a wife's contribution to a marriage
and distributed property inequitably in divorce settlements. Still others
treated the efforts of women to obtain and enforce child-support awards
as unimportant.

"More is found in this examination of gender bias in the courts than
bruised feelings resulting from rude or callous behavior," the 313-page
report concluded. "Women uniquely, disproportionately and with un-
acceptable frequency must endure a climate of condescension, indifference and hostility."

The Task Force recommended a series of actions. It urged the Chief
Judge of the Court of Appeals, Sol Wachtler (successor to Judge Law-
rence H. Cooke, who set up the panel) to name a special assistant with
the sole responsibility of monitoring discrimination against women, in-
vestigating complaints and setting up a training program to make judges
less biased in their dealings with women.

The panel also called on the New York State Legislature to enact
laws that better protect women in cases involving child custody and
family violence. It also urged bar associations and law schools to con-
duct programs on discrimination against women in the courts and on
the rights of women in rape cases and family disputes.

By and large women are the losers in court battles for divorce, custody and the amount of dollars awarded because of the attitudes of
judges. In New York the Equitable Distribution Law has been passed
giving women a right to a part of the property or money amassed during
the marriage. But women who have been married many years or who
have many children often do not get the money they need and may be
forced to sell the house in which they live to meet current expenses.
Usually, in divorce cases, a man's economic situation is improved and
a wife's greatly impaired when there are children.

An editorial in *The New York Times* on August 8, 1986, headed "Re-
balancing the Divorce Scale," started off: "A funny thing happens to
many women when their marriages end. Often, within the first year of
divorce, their standard of living is apt to drop. That of their former husbands is apt to rise. To relieve such inequity, Governor [Mario] Cuomo
recently signed several amendments to New York's divorce law. To correct such inequity, several more are needed."

New York was one of the last states to hold that the person named on the savings account, the deed and other assets, was the one who got to keep them and almost always that person was the husband, the editorial said.

Today an important question has been raised—would the world have more of a chance for peace if women were given more voice in deciding the issues of war and peace? Would there be less focus on weapons, more on achieving statesmanship in leaders and among nations by setting up a powerful international organization composed of men and women to serve as arbiter when nations disagreed?

"Where are the women?" asks Betty G. Lall, a political economist, referring to women at the forefront where nuclear arms control is concerned. Director of Urban Affairs and Public Policy Program at Cornell University, she was named by UNESCO as one of the world's three leading women experts on arms control.

She wrote in an article, "The Nuclear Threat, a Woman's Perspective," in *On the Issues,* published by the Women's Medical Center of Forest Hills, New York, in the spring of 1986: "It is an interesting fact that women have been shunted aside when high-level discussions turn to issues of armament—especially interesting since women have been at the forefront as activists where nuclear arms control is concerned. Yet when push comes to shove, we are the ones being shoved—away from the negotiating table."

She added, "There is no question that throughout history, with few exceptions, it has been men not women who prepare for and wage wars. If women are not a part of policy-making decisions, what can we do? We can speak out and know that we are not alone. There are millions waiting for our courage."

She maintains that if women take part actively in the national debate, "using both knowledge and common sense," they can make the difference in whether the United States moves safely toward arms control or another futile, perhaps disastrous to the world, war.

Incidentally, rage has led some women into roles where their courage played an important part. Deborah Sampson of Plympton, Massachusetts, only a few miles from Plymouth where the first settlers landed, became the first woman to fight in the American Army—during the Revolution. Disguised as a man, during the last two years of the war, she chose this dangerous mission in large part driven by an unconscious rage because her father had early abandoned his family and she was farmed out to a farmer's family where she did all the chores. At the age of nineteen, after all the sons of the farmer had left home to fight in the Army, she dressed in a masculine outfit she had sewn, cut her hair short, walked from Boston to West Point, New York, with a group of soldiers to fight the Redcoats in Westchester County. She was wounded in the thigh by a bullet but removed it herself, fearing her identity as a woman would be discovered if taken to a doctor.

As the war ended, Deborah was part of a troop that rode horseback from West Point to Philadelphia where American soldiers were staging an uprising against Congress because they had received no pay for months. The uprising was halted but Deborah caught the flu, which was an epidemic, and was taken unconscious to a hospital. There a doctor discovered her secret. He did not tell anyone but wrote a letter for her to carry back to her commander at West Point in which he disclosed the fact that this "soldier" was a woman. The commander was stunned but the war was over by this time, he had become fond of the "man" Deborah had portrayed (she had taken her dead brother's name, Robert Shurtlief) and decided to send her home with all his good wishes. She later became the first woman to be granted a pension for serving in the Army.

Deborah Sampson then fulfilled what is thought the "mission" of a woman by marrying and bearing children. She also became a lecturer on her experiences during the war. In Rock Ridge Cemetery in Sharon, Massachusetts, where she lived after she was married for the rest of her life, her gravestone holds the inscription:

> Deborah Sampson Gannett
> Robert Shurtlief
> The Female Soldier
>
> Service 1781–1783

She is the only woman in this country to have a Revolutionary Grave Marker. In the middle of the village green at Plympton, where she was born, a bronze plaque in her honor on a boulder reads: "In honor of Deborah Sampson who for love of country served Two years as a soldier with WAR OF THE REVOLUTION."

Deborah Sampson had made up her mind one night when she was nineteen, driven by angers of the past and a strong wish she had been born a boy, to fight for her country. Her courage was admirable at that time in the nation's history, though today women are marshaling their rage to fight for peace.

Unlike men, women experience their aggressive wishes and strivings as a major threat rather than a basis for self-esteem. This occurs because parents hold different expectations of sons and daughters, behave differently toward them. As a result, a girl's assertiveness may be expressed quite differently and in different intensity than a boy's.

Little girls gain the start of self-esteem through their parents. The little girl consciously and unconsciously accepts her mother and father's value of her (and of themselves). If she lives with constant humiliation and demeaning by her parents, her image of herself will be poor. If her parents demean each other, she absorbs this feeling about herself as she identifies with them. As she moves along in her emotional development, she takes in her parents' values, attitudes and fantasies, always adding fantasies of her own created out of her unique experiences. No two persons have exactly the same life experiences though their emotions may be the same about the experiences.

Many little girls think sadly, "Oh, if I were only a boy!" They are influenced by the godlike way their mothers and fathers treat a brother. One young woman grew up with four older brothers. Margaret Solow, a writer, who lives in Los Angeles, recalls friends would say to her in earlier years, "Oh, you must be so spoiled, with four older brothers." But, she adds, "I felt quite the contrary. I was the lowest in the pecking order. When I was younger the boys would pick on me, tease me, though they never physically hurt me."

She admired her four brothers, wanted to be like them. She dressed in slacks, jeans, pants, wore her brothers' old army jackets, refused to learn to sew or how to cook, the "womanly" chores. But she finally discovered she liked "being daddy's little girl," and came to terms with her femininity. Her father is Dr. Robert S. Solow, noted child psychiatrist in Beverly Hills.

Many little girls wish to be boys, believing boys have the power, are loved better. The fantasy of being a "changeling," of undergoing a metamorphosis that will bring happiness and power reveals the wish of little girls and women to be transformed into men. It is the fantasy of many a woman that she can transform herself into something else, usually a more sexy, more beautiful being. This is the adult version of the little girl's wish to turn from an ugly duckling into a graceful swan. According to *Webster's New World Dictionary*, a *changeling* is "a child secretly put in the place of another; any ugly, queer, idiotic or bad-tempered child, superstitiously explained away as being a substitute child left by the fairies for a child stolen by them."

The little girl may have this fantasy in reverse. She believes she was stolen from her rightful parents and forced to live with "ugly, queer, idiotic or bad-tempered" parents, and that her real mother and father were of noble origin, wealthy and, in addition, warm and loving. This, in Freud's words, is "the family romance." It holds the little girl's very strong wish to deny what she thinks are her parents' cruelty and indifference to her, and her subsequent rage and guilt. If she is a changeling, or if they are not her real parents, she need not feel guilty about either her sexual or aggressive wishes toward them.

One little girl stormed at her mother, "I don't have to obey you. You're not my *real* mother."

The mother was at first shocked, then amused. She asked, "Who do you think is your real mother?"

"Mrs. Cunningham," said the little girl, naming the mother of her best friend. "She's *always* nice to me."

"But Mrs. Cunningham is Grace's mother," said the girl's mother.

"She's mine, too," insisted the little girl. "*She* never yells at me. Or orders me around. Or punishes me."

The idea of becoming part of someone else's family, of turning into a different kind of child or gaining another sort of parent, is carried over into adulthood in those women who unconsciously seek in a man the accepting, kind, thoughtful parent they believe they lacked as a little girl. Such women expect marriage to solve all their conflicts, look on their husbands not as human beings, with all the faults of a human being, but as the "perfect" parent they lacked.

Along with the changeling fantasy goes the rescue fantasy. Both stem from the little girl's wish that someone strong will come along to rescue her from her wretched parents. Some women live as though this fantasy were still possible to achieve, waiting for Prince Charming to magically appear and help them find the answers to life in eternal happiness.

The woman who must be the rescuer, who keeps busy by helping other people out of their misery, in one sense is showing her strong wish to be rescued. Her act of "rescuing" in part masks the underlying wish to save herself from torment. She is saying to those she rescues, "I am doing unto you what I wish were done unto me."

St. Thomas Aquinas called woman "a misbegotten male." Centuries later, after observing and listening to male patients, and delving into his own unconscious, Freud said he believed man's treatment of women as inferior masked man's own inner terror each time he looked at the body of a woman and realized it lacked a penis. This aroused his deepest fear—castration. His contempt of the female body arose in defense against that fear.

Women themselves accepted this masculine bias until recently. They even outdid men in depreciation of women, thereby colluding in their own age-old subjugation. Out of her feelings of inferiority woman envies and fears man's sexual and physical power. She submits to him out of that fear, then feels an underlying contempt for him, as he does for her.

In matriarchal societies women have tried to dominate as they imitate the overthrown, psychologically castrated males and assumed power. Rather than treat men as their partners, the Amazons openly sought to defeat and subjugate them, unlike most women who, over the centuries, hid their desire for revenge. We might question whether Joan of Arc went to war primarily in the interest of saving her country or whether, unconsciously, she wanted to slaughter the enemy man, for only men were warriors in those days.

How a daughter feels about having children is related to the attitude of her mother—how she saw her mother act with her and her siblings. If her mother gave the message children were "trouble," interfered with her life, could cause her "to drop dead," as one mother threatened her son and daughter when they misbehaved ("You'll be the death of me!") a daughter is not likely to look upon having children with much joy.

How a mother values herself determines in large part how her daughter will value herself. A thirty-two-year-old psychoanalytic patient, speaking of her shaky sense of self-worth, said to her therapist, "I grew up feeling sorry for my mother, who was always feeling sorry for herself. I don't think she ever had much sense of being valued by my father or by herself."

She added bitterly, "My father walked out on her after ten years of marriage for another woman. After that she sank into a deep depression and has never come out of it."

This daughter, as a result of her treatment, possesses a growing sense of self-esteem her mother never had. She has become able to accept her buried rage and at last realizes her mother and father did the best they could in view of the lives they had endured. The daughter has tried to persuade her mother also to seek help but her mother says adamantly, "There's nothing wrong with *me*. It's your father. He's caused my misery." The daughter understands that her mother is unable to start the search within that is difficult but, if successful, diminishes the torment of life.

A daughter, in growing up, will absorb emotionally from her mother the feeling either that a woman is inferior or is as esteemed and valued as a man. The daughter also gains a sense of herself from her father and how he treats the women in the family. Though essentially it is the mother the daughter uses as role model and if the mother respects herself, the daughter will respect both her mother and herself.

The less angry the mother, the less angry the daughter. Anger hides behind depression so we can also say the less depressed the mother, the less depressed the daughter.

As daughters can accept assertion as their right, they will raise more emotionally adjusted daughters and sons. It is likely that more of the daughters of today's women will not think of aggression as a condemnatory word, as their mothers and grandmothers did, but accept it as most men do—for use in daily activities, in creativity, in exploring the world, in achieving, be it on the job or in words and deeds aimed at world peace.

6 🎵 Rage in Men

Over the centuries men have appeared to display their anger and hostility to a far greater degree than women. Men have committed far more murders, been openly far more sadistic and vengeful. Men have been the plunderers, the pirates, the rapists, the invaders of other nations, the ones who decided whether countries went to war. Men have possessed the power to set the laws and customs, including those that applied to women, such as the right to have abortions.

Yet men have suffered as much as women in an emotional sense, as Dr. Reuben Fine points out in his recent book *The Forgotten Man, Understanding the Male Psyche.* In his preface Fine states that in the extensive literature on human and sexual liberation there is one startling omission, "The psychology of the man."

He declares, "It has been all too generally assumed that men are strong, domineering, ruthless, powerful and perfectly able to take care of themselves." He adds, "Little could be further from the truth. Men are all too often weak, submissive, passive, helpless, dependent and depressed."

He tries in this book to fill in "the gap in the literature of the two sexes," for he feels the conflicts of the man "have been largely overlooked."

He says that "as every psychotherapist knows, men have just as many sexual problems as women" as well as aggressive problems. The cultural ideal of the "macho he-man, with John Wayne as prototype, is in sharp contrast to the analytic ideal of the loving man," Fine points out.

While women numerically appear as the most depressed gender, the highest suicide rate is found among single men over forty-five, he notes, while in people over eighty, the suicide rate is reported to be sixteen times as high in men as women.

He cites "the achievement motive" in men as powerful, "yet paradoxically, the net psychological outcome is frequently to instill a feeling of failure in the man because he has not achieved enough." Nor is success any guarantee of happiness, he adds, pointing to very wealthy men and women who have committed suicide or landed in mental hospitals.

Fine calls Thoreau's remark that most men lead lives "of quiet desperation" a "very apt one."

He points to the fact that men as boys are taught not to cry when they are hurt or to make any public display of emotion. In the light of the experiences of psychoanalysts, there is no particular reason, he says, "to suppose that men are more logical or rational than women. Thus the effort to keep up with the masculine ideal creates a misperception of both the man and the woman."

It has been made very clear, Fine says, that there is a wide gap between the masculine ideal that serves as a model for most boys as they grow up and the "analytic ideal" that has evolved from the careful study of neurosis and psychosis over the past one hundred years. The "forgotten man" is more often than not on the horns of a dilemma: "If he behaves the way real he-men are supposed to, he suppresses his feelings, blocks off his affection, releases his rage and aggression, strives for success by fair means or foul—and takes the consequences."

One important consequence is lifelong depression and misery, accompanied by innumerable other illnesses. Charles Revson, who built up a one-hundred-million-dollar fortune from nothing, once said, "What's there to say about my life? It's just miserable." He would not seek a psychoanalyst, talk of why he felt so miserable.

On the other hand, if the man admits to his fears and failings he suffers in another way, "since such a stigma is attached to not being a true he-man," Fine explains. In a man's choices during his lifetime he is guided "more by some mythical image of what a man should be like than by the realities of the situation." Tenderness is regarded as "feminine," being a "sissy."

Fine says one of the problems is that men "live for victory, they want to be the best, the strongest, win at any cost." This means many will feel frustrated, then enraged when they cannot reach the top, gain the honor of being "the fastest gun in the west."

Many men are sadistic to women as they let out on a wife the fury they never dared show as boys to their overpossessive, dictating mothers. Homosexuals are known for the physical damage they inflict on their "feminine" partners, who, in their unconscious, become temporarily the "bad mother" of childhood.

As Elia Kazan, the famous director of films and plays, writes in his eloquent, moving autobiography, A Life, "Men, I've found, despite their swagger and bravado, are far less sure of themselves than women and need more affirmation and support. The competition through which they have to make their way is more intense, often brutal. Witness their locker room boasts about deals, scores, victories, and sexual triumphs."

He states that the actresses with whom he has worked are better artists because their feelings are concerned with their intimate life. "Men have to be constantly proving something that is not often worth proving—their muscles, their fearlessness, their affluence, the strength of their erections," he says.

Rage in men starts the same way as rage in women—with the very early relationship to the mother. The degree of rage a man feels depends on a mother's love and care and her ability to allow her little son slowly to start emotional separation from her at nine months of age. If a mother is overprotective, overdominating, overdemanding, or if she is critical or noncaring, he will find it difficult to gain an identity of his own, too tightly tied to her emotionally.

At no time of life is more viability given a boy "than during the early thralldom years of a little boy's intimacy with his mother," says Dr. Gregory Rochlin in *The Masculine Dilemma*. "For our search as to what is the matrix of masculinity, it is very important."

If a mother is a single parent of a son, particular emotional conflicts arise, he points out. Their mutual problems tend to become "invariably intensified. What for the son is ordinarily a transient conflict with regard to his mother becomes prolonged." Rochlin mentions particularly "identification with his mother."

A mother also affects her young son's development "when she seductively presses him toward ambitious achievement that unconsciously expresses her needs more than his," Rochlin says. "Despite the assurances of his success, there are also wishes to fail and thus be relieved of the obligation to his mother."

The roots of homosexuality lie in childhood, psychoanalysts believe. They are fostered by a number of strong fantasies. They include the wish to be like the mother, think like the mother, never lose the mother. There is also great rage at the mother, for in her threats of punishment the boy fantasizes she will take his penis away and he will have left only the dark, empty hole little girls possess.

Rochlin says there is general agreement among all who have studied the unconscious structure of homosexuality that this development in a man "lies in the persistence of the early-formed and unmodified identification with one's mother. It is assumed that the relationship that may have existed during the child's first year and a half somehow persists unaltered. The adult homosexual man, it is supposed, carries this arrested condition forward from his nursery."

The psychoanalytic studies of men show that the nucleus of the wish to be desired by another man in the way one might be desired by him as a woman, normally is repressed in the average man's unconscious. But if a lasting, unmodified identification of a man with his mother is retained, such a man "is prone to be sexually attracted to another man who would wish to play a woman's role."

Freud's original explanation, with which most current psychoanalysts agree, is that the homosexual remains unconsciously fixated on his mother, to a "mnemic image of her" (she is held fast in his memory). He runs from women who might cause him to be unfaithful to his mother. He pursues or prefers men to whom he has transferred interest from his mother. Freud said, "He hastens to transfer the excitation he has received from women on to a male object, and in this manner he repeats over and over again the mechanism by which he acquired his homosexuality."

Rochlin talks of "transient episodes of depression" that occur in daily life if a man feels slighted, neglected, disappointed and abused—all emotions opposed to love or affection, such as anger, hostility and wishes that flow from these feelings. Such experiences as related to someone with whom intimacy exists and dependency and love have been established, "bring on inescapable, hostile self-judgments that are not readily reversed," he says.

Rochlin disagrees with Freud as to the function of the "latency" period, which begins about the end of a boy's fifth year and lasts until the first signs of puberty. Freud called this a time of relative freedom from conflict following the dénouement of the oedipus complex. Rochlin refers to this period as "boyhood" and describes it as "an active phase launched in earnest." It is, he says, "a time of notoriously aggressive pursuits that have as their chief, unconscious aims the reconditioning of the battered ego of failed wishes and painful limitations from the earlier phrase," with an activation of the aggressive pursuit "to restore the masculine ego."

Incidentally, the transvestite wishes his penis removed so he will physically resemble a woman and he can dress like a woman to identify more completely with the mother of childhood. "The hazard for the boy lies in that he not only identifies with his mother's femininity but he also retains it," Rochlin explains. "Moreover, he perceives that he is the carrier of her masculine wishes that she would have fulfilled through him." In other words, he represents the strong masculine part of a woman unable to be fully feminine, who wishes she were a man.

Freud said, speaking of homosexuality, "If a person of the opposite sex is available, why should a male choose another male or a female another female . . . over even, sometimes, a lock of hair or a piece of underclothing?" The answer is to be found, he believed, in how the man develops emotionally from the day he is born in relation to his mother.

Freud explained that originally our sexual instinct is independent of its object, that our "libido," which at first was, in his words, "polymorphous perverse"—meaning it does not differentiate between the sexes—undergoes development and integration when we are children. It passes through a homosexual phase before reaching the heterosexual level. As a result of the "early psychic trauma," which "prevents the person from proceeding to the heterosexual stage," he will feel enraged.

In his book *Homosexuality*, Dr. Charles W. Socarides, well-known psychoanalyst, explains that the homosexual "drains off into a psychic masochistic state the aggressive assaultiveness toward the mother and, secondarily, toward the father. All homosexuals deeply fear the knowledge that their homosexual acts constitute an eroticized defense against a more threatening masochistic state. Libidinal and aggressive impulses against the mother and father lead to masochistic wishes which then seek effective discharge through the homosexual relationship."

Masochism (in which we take the beating instead of administering it and showing our anger) is not only a method of neutralizing aggression but of keeping the tie to the mother. The homosexual wants to escape the all-powerful, punitive or seductive acts of the mother but he does not dare cease being her thinly disguised "slave," needing desperately what love he can get from her.

In the masochistic state, guilt over incestuous feelings for the mother is continually bought off through self-punitive activities. The pain in masochism, which is self-induced and self-controlled, gives rise to a false sense of victory, elation and omnipotence. For the moment, the man feels in a "state of masochistic invulnerability."

The homosexual will claim he is not masochistic, that he chooses a way of life he prefers. Socarides says, "Nevertheless, in reality he is unconsciously committed to and captured by his need to avoid what he fears would be extinction due to the tremendous threat of maternal engulfment.

"To fortify himself and to make himself secure against this possibility," he "aggrandizes, elevates and romanticizes his variant sexual activity. Masochism is not to be defeated; even in the course of his homosexual pleasure, masochism prevails."

He concludes, "Orgastic activity and pleasure partially and temporarily relieve the tendency toward regression and toward the powerful masochistic state which, were it to get out of hand, would threaten his psychic survival."

Because the homosexual must forego his striving for gratification of his intense attachment to his mother (and, consequently to other women), as well as his closeness to his father, he experiences severe feelings of loneliness throughout life.

"Homosexuality is an attempt to achieve human contact and to break through stark isolation. The homosexual claims that this motivation is to find love but in many instances this is merely a rationalization for the overriding and imperative need for neutralization of anxiety through homosexual orgastic contact," Socarides explains. The loneliness "is in reality an acute, intense depression mixed with mounting anxiety which threatens his psychological equilibrium if sexual contact is not made quickly." One of the homosexual's many fantasies is that through sexual unity with a man, he becomes a man.

The rage within the homosexual is seen in the many vicious attacks made on male partners during or after the act of sex. Even murders of homosexual partners occur, as well as bloody attacks and mutilation of the body. The early "cannibalistic" feelings of the baby at times overcome the homosexual as he displays his rage at his partner.

That the stereotypes of man and woman still persist was clearly shown in an article in *The New York Times* on June 15, 1989, which was titled: "Toys: Girls Still Apply Makeup, Boys Fight Wars." The reporter, Carol Lawson, stated that in families across the country it is "toys as usual: girls are playing with frilly dolls that have man-luring manes and awesome wardrobes, and boys are playing with armed action figures that stand ready to battle for control of the universe."

The feminist revolution may have reshaped a number of derogatory areas of a woman's life but it has failed to reach into the early years of the child—important years in determining the later maturity of the boy or girl.

Leaders of the women's movement envisioned more than a decade ago rearing children with toys that were not necessarily stereotyped by gender. Toy manufacturers claim the notion of breaking down sex barriers in toys has failed because boys and girls have distinct play patterns that do not waver.

"Girls' play involves dressing and grooming and acting out their future—going on a date, getting married—and boys' play involves competition and conflict, good guys versus bad guys," explained Glenn Bozarth, director of public relations for Mattel Inc., which makes the Barbie doll.

According to child development experts and parents there is pressure from children's peers, plus a barrage of toy advertisements on Saturday morning television, which reinforce sex stereotypes. Some parents also refer to an uneasiness in society over encouraging boys to play with toys other than those traditionally associated with masculinity.

Dr. Bruno Bettelheim, famous child psychologist, believes children do not possess an innate need for particular kinds of toys. He says, "I don't think it is very important for them to play with gender-stereotyped toys. Children should be free to play with whatever toys they want."

Today there are even more aggressive toys for boys, such as GI Joe figures, men holding all kinds of destructive weapons, army tanks, grinning, weird figures from outer space. From an early age, a boy will have embedded in his mind the image of "man" as a cruel, killer-type person.

The vision of a man as cruel and uncaring, bent on destroying others, persists in the unconscious. Many men are able to keep from acting out this hidden rage but there are also hundreds of thousands throughout the world who daily explode in rage, either at strangers, members of their own family, or the wife and children they have acquired through marriage.

As Fine said, quoted earlier, the "psychology of man" is missing from our thinking. Man is trained early in life to hold back tears, to be warlike, to treat women as the inferior sex. Perhaps until both men and women can accept the same vulnerabilities in men as in women, equality in full will be denied women as a way of men saying, "Help us, too, realize how we are not fully able to become a man, in the full sense of the word, and then we will help you become more fully 'equal.'"

7 ⬤ Rage in Sex and Marriage

Most of us grow up with the fantasy that someday we will meet "the right person." Someone who will be perfect for us, who will fill the rest of our life with constant love and joy. We do not believe our feelings or the other person's could ever change. Marriage means "forever."

But the statistics prove us wrong. A report on the divorce figures for 1986 compiled by the National Center for Health Statistics, a division of the Federal Department of Health and Human Services, showed that 1,178,000 marriages broke up that year throughout the nation. This statistic appeared in *The New York Times* on June 15, 1989. The all-time high occurred in 1981 when a total of 1,213,000 men or women filed divorces.

The report revealed that when a marriage in this country ended in divorce, the wife was nearly twice as likely as the husband to initiate the process. Women filed 61.5 percent of the divorce petitions acted on in 1986 and men filed 32.6 percent. The remaining petitions were filed jointly.

Among couples with children, women filed 65.7 percent of the divorce petitions. Among childless couples, women initiated 56.7 percent. Traditionally, women have predominated in filing for divorce. Divorces also were most likely to occur early in marriage, with 33.6 percent taking place in the fourth year. Over all, marriages that ended in divorce lasted an average of 9.6 years. First marriages that ended in divorce lasted 10.7 years while second marriages ended after 6.7 years and third marriages lasted 7.2 years.

Why do so many marriages fail? According to psychoanalysts, because so many men and women expect the impossible of the one they marry. They expect him to be the perfect parent they never had. The fantasy of "romantic love," felt as man and woman first meet in a crowded room or aboard an airplane or on a vacation ship at sea, seldom lasts. Soon each sees the other without rose-colored glasses and discovers the other cannot live up to expectations.

It is then that hatred fills the air. We expect to be rescued from our rage of the past, not feel it even more intensely. But the burdens that marriage imposes, the suffocating closeness that leads to limiting our freedom to "be," takes a toll of romantic love. Disillusionment and anger quickly follow.

Perhaps one reason a harmonious marriage is very unusual in our society, according to Dr. Herbert S. Strean in *The Extramarital Affair*, is that "there is a lack of understanding of why mates select each other." He points out that the psychological factors involved in choosing a mate "are more difficult to describe than social variables because they are subtle and unconscious."

Though most men and women think of their choice of a marital partner as a result of "free, rational choice," psychoanalysts emphasize that strong, unconscious feelings and wishes motivate our choice of mate.

According to psychoanalytic theory, "mate choice is never an accident, the prospective marital partners are always influenced by unconscious and frequently irrational motives," Strean states. "When marriages founder, it is usually not because the couple has incompatible interests but because they are ignorant of the unconscious purposes that determined their respective choices."

In Romeo's words, love is "A madness most discreet, / A choking gall, and a preserving sweet." The "madness most discreet" is a state of passionate love that psychoanalysts have compared to a psychosis where reality is obliterated as the man or woman lives temporarily in a dreamworld. "Choking gall" describes the intense agony the lover feels when he or she feels rejected. Yet, love is a "preserving sweet," in that the warm feelings between lovers sustain and nurture them, Strean explains. That is, until reality starts to set in and all passion may vanish.

One important aspect of the connection between our sexual feelings and rage arose in Freud's mind early in his career. In a letter written January 16, 1899, to his friend, Dr. Wilhelm Fliess, to whom he expressed all his findings as he built the science of psychoanalysis, Freud explained that the hysterical headaches of which his first patients—all women—complained "are due to a fantastic parallel which equates the head with the other end of the body (hair in both places—cheeks and buttocks—lips and labiae—mouth and vagina): so that a migraine can be used to represent a forcible defloration, the illness thus standing for a wish-fulfillment. That the sexual is the conditioning factor stands out with ever-increasing clarity."

He then described a patient "whom I cured with the help of the phantasy key," who had been "continually plunged into despair by the gloomy conviction that she was useless, good for nothing, etc. I always thought that in early childhood she must have seen her mother in a similar state, in an attack of real melancholia." He added, "it now turns out that at the age of fourteen she," the patient, "discovered an *atresia hymenalis* in herself and despaired of ever being able to function fully as a woman."

Freud concluded, "Melancholia is thus fear of impotence. Similar states in which she could not make up her mind to choose a hat or a dress go back to the time when she had to choose her husband."

He spoke of another case in which an "important and wealthy" man, a bank director, came to see him to talk about the peculiarities of a young girl who was his mistress. Freud said he "threw out the guess" that she was probably "quite anaesthetic," then learned, on the contrary, she was able to have from four to six orgasms during a single coitus.

But she fell into a "tremor" as soon as the bank director approached her and immediately after coitus fell into a pathological sleep in which she talked as though under hypnosis, later had complete amnesia about what she said. Freud told Fliess, "He will marry her off and she will certainly be anaesthetic towards her husband. Her elderly lover, because of the easy identification with the powerful father of her childhood, obviously affects her in such a way as to release the libido attached to her phantasies. Very instructive!"

In another letter written shortly thereafter, on February 19, 1899, he spoke of a new finding, saying, "It is not only dreams that are fulfillments of wishes, but hysterical attacks as well. . . . It probably applies to every product of neurosis—for I recognized it long ago in actual delusional insanity."

He then wrote lines that have become famous: "Reality—wish-fulfillment; it is from this contrasting pair that our mental life springs." He went on, "I believe I now know the determining condition which distinguishes dreams from symptoms that force their way into waking life."

He explained: "It is enough for a dream to be the wish-fulfillment of the repressed thought; for a dream is kept apart from reality. But a symptom, which has its place in actual life, must be something else as well—the wish-fulfillment of the *repressing* thought. A symptom arises where the repressed and the repressing thoughts can come together in the fulfillment of a wish. A symptom, in its character of a punishment, for instance, is a wish-fulfillment of the repressing thought, while self-punishment is the final substitute for self-gratification—for masturbation."

Freud gave an example, saying, "Here we have the key to many problems. Do you know, for instance, why X.Y. suffered from hysterical vomiting? Because in her imagination she is pregnant, because she is so insatiable that she cannot do without having a baby even from her last imaginary lover. But she also vomits because then she will be starved and emaciated, will lose her looks and cease to attract anyone. Thus the meaning of the symptom is the fulfillment of a pair of contradictory wishes."

Freud compared this to "a clever work of fiction," saying, "and yet how characteristic of 'man with all his contradictions'!"

While at this early stage in his formulations Freud did not emphasize rage, or "the aggressive impulse," he did refer to hate as arising from many feelings and events in a person's life. But he gave the sexual instinct and the many complicated emotions attached to it sole responsibility for the suffering that ensued from childhood on and led to neurosis or psychosis.

Each gender experiences certain rages at the other for not "understanding" his or her needs, often hurls the sarcastic words, "You're not a man!" or "You're not a woman!" at the partner. There is little that wounds a man or woman more deeply than to be denigrated in this sensitive psychic area.

Many women find it difficult, if not impossible, to be nurturers to their husbands for they were not nurtured sufficiently as children. Many men are not "gallant" or "understanding" or even wish to remain faithful to a wife because they did not have loving, understanding, faithful parents.

As a marriage breaks up each feels the other "does not give me all I need"—an impossible demand. The need is based on childhood longings for the tenderness and caring that was lacking at that time. No one can make up for this, it has to be accepted before the cry for it can cease.

Marriage starts to become difficult after the honeymoon as both partners begin to feel the stir of rage when, in some way, the other does something that embarrasses him or her, or goes against a strong belief or belittles him or her. The partner somehow arouses a memory or memories of the past when someone in the person's life behaved the same way and caused him or her to feel denigrated.

It is no longer, "How do I love thee? Let me count the ways," but "How do I hate you? Let me count the ways."

A twenty-five-year-old bride of six months told her mother sadly, "How could I have been so blind in not knowing what Jack was like before marrying him? He seemed so considerate, so gentle, so sexual. Then shortly following our honeymoon he started to show a Mr. Hyde side after two scotches. He would scream at me, sometimes slap me if I did what he considered the slightest wrong."

She sighed, went on, "I can't understand what he wants and I know he cannot, or does not want to understand me." Added, "And I'm afraid of him. Last night he got very drunk and hit me so hard I fell on the floor."

Her mother said, "You have to leave him. He's dangerous."

"I know that," the daughter agreed. "But he's always so apologetic in the morning. Says he didn't know what he was doing after a stiff drink."

But she did leave him a month later when she found herself in a hospital following his striking her so severely she lost consciousness. She went to an analyst to discover why she had unconsciously chosen such a brutal mate.

Another wife of twenty-seven discovered her new husband became impotent following a month of what she described to a friend as "listless sex, as if he didn't really care." He blamed her for not being passionate enough to raise his sexual desire, saying angrily, "Before I married you I had a lot of women and there were no complaints."

Psychoanalysts know that when men become impotent in marriage (or out of marriage) this sexual fear is tied in fantasy to the childhood oedipal fear of taking mother from father. Or the fear of a mother, who has been too seductive or its opposite, that she has made her small son feel his growing love for her is "indecent," "wrong," because she fears her sexual feelings for him.

For centuries it was believed that a wife, in the sexual sense, was present in bed to gratify a man's need for sexual expression. But today many women believe they deserve equality in bed as well as in the workplace and the political scene. This has led some men to maintain women are "aggressive sexually" when they are only trying to be considered an equal partner.

Sexual liberation, part of the feminist movement, is not however achieved by the wave of a magic wand that brings immediate gratification of childhood fantasies (real and unreal). Such as the granting of every sexual wish or the use of sex as a release of anger and anxiety. When a sexual relationship is asked to make up for the lack of pleasure in other areas or to serve as cloak for the impossible dreams of child-hood, it can only fail.

Sexual liberation is part of the aura of what Dr. Herbert Hendin, a pioneer in the application of psychoanalysis to the study of contempo-rary society, titles his book—*The Age of Sensation.* He studied a number of college students and concluded that vulnerability in every corner of life exists in the feelings of anger shown by both the women and men students.

He said of the women students he interviewed, "The fury in most young women I saw, drawn at random from the college population, bright, lively young people, was caused by these women seeing life as a series of dangers they wanted to avoid."

They had grown up after the sexual revolution; independence in work was their common goal, he said. They did not "politicize" their situation as women, "nor define male oppression as the social factor they had to overcome." Nor did they focus on the emotional damage of the past, though many had endured painful childhoods.

"What they pursued with all their available energy was an emotion-free oasis where neither love, nor anger, nor depression could touch them," he observed. Describing the young women as believing they were totally in charge of their lives in the hope they could become the roles they play, he added, "What they often achieve is a distance from the sources of their own unhappiness so great that some would begin to cry without knowing why while they told me about the lives they said were perfect."

These young women "were determined not to get hurt, not to fall into what many saw as the deception of marriage and the snare of moth-erhood," which they regarded as "the final seal on the marital trap." They saw, he said, "any deep involvement with men as inevitably de-structive. Some avoided anything but casual dating, insisting that any sexual or romantic attachment means inevitable pain. Most preferred friendships with occasional sex to the intense intimacy of love."

For these young women, men were not political enemies nor sexual tools, nor "exactly people either. Relations with men were the battle-ground on which these young women fought against their own vulnera-bility," Hendin commented. Work, as the barrier against need, as the testing ground of individual worth, as the best defensive weapon, was "very much in the minds of these young women. Those unable to form strong interest in a career were tormented, believing that they would be doomed to wretched and unhappy lives."

He gave the example of one sophomore student who imagined what her life would be in ten years and wrote two versions. In one she was single, happy and pursuing a career she liked. In the other, she was trapped by screaming children, miserably married. He commented, "She was typical in her feeling that life was divided between unencumbered happiness at work and total self-destruction in motherhood and marriage. She quietly predicted she would have the worse fate because she had no strong work interest to shield her." He added, "The self-protective significance of work was dramatized by the many women I saw who used it to forge an emotional armor."

These young women lacked confidence that they could enter into any intimate relationship with a man, set limits and survive happily. They remained "on perpetual alert," he said, against anything that might interfere with the work to which they tied their entire emotional lives. The woman fled bondage to a man, bondage to the mother of childhood, thinking of herself as slave to her mother, slave to the man she married.

The young women looked on their mothers' lives as examples of what to avoid, not emulate. They feared engulfment and being submerged, like their mothers, and dealt with such vulnerability by trying to avoid the same fate. Their freedom to be involved with men was not accompanied by confidence in their ability to protect themselves when they became involved. Their emotional state was made still more difficult by the escalation of aggression against them in the young men who feared that women now demanded more of men sexually and otherwise. Such young women, in the search for an "antidote to emotion," Hendin says, "often find they have killed their power to care deeply for anyone."

In describing his interviews with the young men students, he reported they also withdrew from being aware of their emotions. They felt a desire "to take as much as they could from life while giving as little as possible of themselves." They saw a relationship to a woman as "combat," did not feel protective to a young woman, did not trust her. Closeness with a woman unleashed their rage, they were quick to slap a girl, pull back from involvements, feared their potential to harm a woman. Summed up Hendin: "It is the sense of anger at the core that shapes them."

To these young men, casual sex seemed the way to deal with conflicts intimacy aroused and the way to express anger toward women without becoming involved. They were unable to feel tenderness or affection, did not seek it, could not accept it if offered. They began tearing a woman down, belittling or abusing her as soon as they were mildly involved. Some treated women cruelly to drive them away. They did not know the source of their anger—the fear a woman would control them as did their dominating mother when they grew up.

"Their own retaliatory impulses to control the woman often keeps such relationships on a seesaw of submission and dominance in which each uses the other to control their aggression," Hendin summed up. "Relationships based on mutual insecurity and mutual reassurance often serve to keep anger in check, but not for long." The men are detached, are afraid of involvement, belittle women. Such reactions, Hendin explains, concentrate only on "personal gratification without concern for anyone else's . . . defense maneuvers that inescapably produce self-hate."

Such relationships, he added, stem the woman's anger for the time being but eventually her aggression is bound to break through and destroy the relationship. In the past most women chose to marry because to remain single carried with it a strong social stigma. An unmarried woman was seen by society as unattractive, unworthy, unwanted. Single women experienced pressure from their parents to marry—the decision they made usually was not whether to marry but whom to marry and as soon as possible.

A recent study of unmarried women and men revealed the reasons for remaining unmarried, all expressed in negative terms: hostility toward marriage or members of the opposite sex, lack of interest in heterosexual partners, emotional involvement with parents, unattractiveness, inability to find "true love," unwillingness to assume responsibility, perception of marriage as a threat to career or economic problems.

"Single in America," another study of the unmarried, gave more positive reasons for choosing to remain single. Both men and women praised the increased freedom and enjoyment of life. They also spoke of chances to meet people and develop friendships, economic independence, more opportunity for personal development. A third study of the single woman in today's society suggested that for a woman's choice to remain single to be successful, she must be economically independent, socially and psychologically autonomous and have a clear preference for the single life.

The changing social and sexual attitudes have also made it possible for both men and women to fulfill their needs for intimate relationships without marriage. Also to take part in a greater range of activities than was possible in the past, such as frequenting places now open to single persons.

Important unconscious reasons exist for not marrying, including anxieties about commitment and sexual intimacy, difficulties in sustaining a relationship and negative feelings about marriage because of early experiences with parents' unhappy relationships. While these reasons may have always existed, the current changes in social patterns and expectations of a woman allow their expression in life choices to a greater degree.

Several studies show the frequency of the intention not to marry. Or show that the postponement of the desired time for marriage increases with more education. One study focused on the characteristics of working single women, including both an age group that was young and uneducated and one that was older and better educated. Many of those in the younger group appeared likely to marry at some later time, whereas many of the more educated, older group appeared likely to remain single and adapt to it.

As one woman of forty-two put it, "If I haven't married by now and find life interesting and exciting—which most of my married woman friends don't, all they do is complain about their dull lives—I am not about to marry now. I don't particularly want children and I have a close man friend who loves me and I love him."

Unforeseen circumstances may also dictate the choice to remain unmarried. Many women have to care for elderly parents or siblings. Others suffer tragedies, such as the loss of a fiancé, and do not wish to look for another man. Some elderly couples do not marry because of economic consideration—they may lose tax benefits or Social Security payments.

Single women report greater freedom and autonomy than married women but they also often find themselves frustrated in their attempts at intimacy and in relationships with men. Many feel socially isolated and lonely. Friendships become an important source of support and sustenance. A number of single women live together or with their parents for emotional or economic support. They are able to put their assertiveness into work and into the relationships they do make and feel life rewarding.

The single woman may find gratification in her self-sufficiency, the choice of an unmarried life may be personally gratifying. Both advantages and disadvantages exist and each woman has to weigh what she wants. For some, the positive aspects of remaining single emerge after an unhappy experience, or experiences, with marriage. Those who are single may decide, later in life, to marry, feeling their single phase has ended or they want to know what it feels like to be married.

Living alone or living with a man without marrying him have become increasingly acceptable options either for a short while or as a life-style, though most single women say they eventually want to marry. The proportion of young singles, particularly women, who establish their own households increased from 21 percent of twenty-five- to thirty-four-year-olds in 1970 to 29 percent in 1975 and is probably higher now, what with the AIDS menace to life.

The number of couples who have made the decision to live together without marrying has also increased considerably in the last decade. Some men and women disapprove of marriage as an institution. Others cite the desire to establish and test a relationship before making a permanent commitment. Loneliness, disillusionment with the superficiality of the "dating game" and the search for intimacy, combined with the reluctance to make a permanent commitment, are also important reasons.

For some couples this arrangement works well, an impetus to further development and maturing. But for others, it becomes a source of anxiety and conflict because the nature of the relationship is not explicit and the fantasized expectations are never realized. Some couples feel committed to each other, see their relationship as similar to marriage, while others are transiently attached or merely share the convenience of housing or cooking.

A twenty-eight-year-old woman, a minor executive in a large advertising agency, told her mother and father, "What difference does it make if Gary and I live together because we love each other and want each other's company or get married? I see too many married couples who split after living together for years. I don't want to take that chance."

Perhaps the mystique of marriage holds additional expectations that often are too great for the woman and man. However the essential point is not marriage or single state but how emotionally mature the partners. How far they have come from the childhood fantasies of demanding the other partner bring happiness, provide all the missing ingredients of life so far.

For some, the nonmarital living situation is a way of working out or testing the relationship before they marry. Their concept of marriage includes a high degree of intimacy and mutual sharing, which they wish to explore before they decide to marry.

The suspending of a commitment is more an issue for women than for men. Men have traditionally expected a woman to adapt to the man's career and life-style. For women, the young adult years have been thought a transitional period from dependence on parents to dependence on a spouse. Women and men who marry early, before they have faced their concerns about identity and independence, may later find their choice of mate inappropriate. Some may be prepared to cope with the tasks of marriage at an early age, others are burdened by their own or their partner's dependency needs and unrealistic expectations, which may destroy the marriage.

In the past a woman's capacity to bear and nurture children gave her a certain self-esteem. While childbearing is an important component of femininity, it is not entirely the central issue. A woman's self-esteem derives in part from this capacity but there are many mothers who are as unhappy as single women. Femininity is a complex, shifting and variable concept, intimately related to the woman's awareness of the capacity to bear and nurture children but not depending on this capacity for her realization as a happy woman.

Feminine development and identity are separate from childbearing. The lack of children does not mean women need feel a sense of failure and inadequacy. Those women who choose not to have children are not necessarily expressing conflict about femininity or an incomplete realization of their feminine potential.

A woman of forty-nine who had a successful career as a concert pianist but never married was for a while very envious of her younger sister who had married at nineteen and raised four children. Then one day the younger sister confessed to her, "I feel like a drudge. My husband no longer seems to appreciate me. The children have left the house and I feel completely alone and abandoned."

The concert pianist said thoughtfully, "I guess each of us made our choices based on what we thought we wanted most. You chose a husband and children, I chose a career. What we chose does not determine whether or not we are feminine. We made our choices as women and they were different ones."

The younger sister looked at her gratefully. "I think you are saying we cannot expect to have it all."

To "have it all" is a childhood wish, only reluctantly given up in adulthood. Each woman senses what she can do best and whether or not she wants to try for "it all." The younger sister might also have had a career, though married, but she undoubtedly felt her children and husband would suffer. The older sister realized the career was all she could handle and preferred that to marriage and raising children. That each differed was related to the unique experiences each had with their mother and father as they grew up and their fantasies of what they wanted most out of life.

Sexual intimacy and the search for the "right" man, who will become part of a lasting relationship, are areas in which women's aggressiveness is tested today. The important question seems to be: Has the so-called sexual revolution really freed women so they are better able to enjoy their sexuality as part of an enduring relationship?

As in all revolutions, there have been some gains, some losses. Old problems are eliminated, new ones emerge. In some ways women have enjoyed new sexual freedoms, both in the finding of partners and in expressing sexual wishes. But if, as men have in the past in regard to women, women now look on men as "sexual objects," they are destined to get little inner joy out of the new liberation. More orgasms perhaps but less self-esteem.

There is a vast difference between sexual "liberation" and sexual "license." True sexual freedom that comes from liberation opens up a woman's capacity to enjoy sex with a lasting partner she loves, respects and trusts, as he does her. Sexual "license" on the other hand, which also involves a "choice," implies a woman is free to have sex with as many partners as she wishes, with no thought of a relationship that includes love, tenderness and respect in addition to sexual release.

Thus the "sexual revolution" may change the name of the game but the underlying conflicts inherent in sexual acting-out when it is apart from love, as in prostitution, remain the same though they appear in different dress. Most of the changes appear in social customs—women alone are permitted to frequent bars, enjoy the haunts of "singles," pick up men as they wish. But no matter how vast the outer changes, if the inner problems remain the same they will pervade the outer facades and anger will prevail.

The new sexual freedom is one aspect of women's liberation from former prohibitions. The new freedom eliminates outer restrictions but it should not be confused with the need to be free of inner restrictions imposed by punitive parental acts in childhood against sexual exploration or expression. Or with the failure in women to understand that reality imposes certain responsibilities when it comes to sexual behavior.

There is a danger in believing all the emotional difficulties of a woman can be eased by sexual liberation. It is a temptation to ignore the inner conflicts, explain them away irrationally in terms of outside forces. But if a woman expects all conflicts to vanish because of the new freedoms, she is due only for disillusionment.

On the plus side in the sexual revolution is the increased awareness in women of their right to enjoy sex as fully as a man does. (This has frightened those men who do not know how to enjoy sex themselves, much less tolerate a woman's enjoying sex.) For centuries women have been expected to serve as the vessel for a man's release of semen, not as participant in an act of pleasure that should be joyous to both. Women were supposed to "submit" to men out of obligation, either as wife or mistress, with the thought, "This is what a man wants, I have no right to my desires or expect they will be fulfilled."

The sexual revolution has won for women, in theory, four gains. The first is that woman is viewed equally as a "person," no longer subject to the derogatory attitudes so prevalent in society. Particularly in America where the wife has so often been described as "the ball and chain," which implies she is a jailer, unreasonable, critical, with a tendency to hold grudges.

The second gain is that woman, at least in theory, has become an "equal sexual partner." She is allowed to initiate sexual activity, expect gratification and announce her sexual preferences. This right has followed her political right to vote and her economic right to be paid equal money with a man on the same job.

The third gain is that women are no longer as dependent upon or enslaved in a marital relationship as in the past. They are now expected to develop skills and be less financially dependent on the man. They are free to use their assertiveness to create, to work, so they no longer feel serflike. The new feminine freedoms have reduced the bondage of the double standard. Woman may now go alone anywhere she chooses, no longer needing a man as guard.

The fourth gain is that woman no longer sees sex as a way a man can exploit her. Ideally, she does not view sexual intercourse as destructive, degrading or soiling. She can exercise more choice of sexual partner. She does not have to accept her role in the sexual relationship as one of passiveness, though her capacity to be passive at times may be part of her sexual allure. Too strident a protest against passivity may lead to pressuring women to be aggressive and competitive in the sexual act, which many men and women find unappealing and distasteful.

True compatibility between a man and a woman implies that neither take out his buried rage on the mate but show love, tenderness and respect for the other. For many men, unfortunately, tenderness, love and respect are believed signs of weakness. There is pressure on a man, internal and external, to appear tough, unfeeling, unsentimental. A number of men have sought to be psychoanalyzed, sensing they repress feelings that torment them, make them angry and depressed. They discover how the denial of their feelings of need and dependency have shaped their lives unhappily.

As they become better able to face and accept the rage, along with the anxiety, guilt and self-hatred they have buried, they move toward a more realistic sense of what it means to be "masculine" and are better able to share a loving relationship with a woman.

Love *is* blind, as the saying goes, when someone does not see his partner as he really is but through those psychically damaging rose-colored glasses. The woman or man who believes life will change from anger and frustration to complete happiness with a new "one and only" after the marriage vow, has monumental expectations so totally unrealistic no one could possibly fulfill them.

Love that is blind has become so in order *not* to see the truth, *not* to feel angry for the moment. Romantic love holds in it a denial of hostile aggression that is inevitably a part of it.

In romantic love there is, according to Dr. Robert Bak, psychoanalyst, an attempt to lose the self in the intensity of the experience and to reinstate the total loving, yearning and fulfillment we as a child experienced in our happiest moments with our mother, fantasizing unity with her.

When such expectations are the goal of a relationship, sooner or later the slightest imperfection or lack of sensitivity shown by the other person will unleash in the partner the rage that lay dormant over the troubled years.

When sex becomes an addiction, in or out of marriage, psychoanalysts have found it holds hostile aggression as well as aggression turned on the self. This occurs because the sexual desire does not arise out of the sharing of passion and love but to fulfill a childhood hunger. Or, as a prostitute uses it, to demean both herself and the man, even though her stated reason is to earn money. Studies have shown that most prostitutes have been abused sexually or violently (or both) as children and as a result it is difficult for them to show understanding, mature love.

Compulsive sex does not always imply promiscuity. One wife insisted her husband have sex every night, whether he felt amorous or sleepy. He complied for three years, then rebelled. She became so angry, she went to a therapist. During her analysis she realized she had been driven by a compulsion that was unfair to her husband. She had demanded nightly proof of his love, in one sense wanting to feel the dominant, powerful one.

If the need for sex is this desperate, the craving is not purely sensual but represents many angry feelings in a man or woman who uses sex for the exploitation of the other person. Some, if they cannot reach orgasm, are furious at their partner as though he or she were present only to serve the partner sexually.

Those who have become aware of buried anger and do not inflict it on a marital partner will, in turn, avoid the unduly hostile partner. They are more sure of their sense of identity, their choice of partner is made on a more mature basis.

A salient point is made by Dr. Robert J. Stoller in *Splitting*. The title refers to a woman's tendency to feel masculine and a man's tendency to feel feminine. He says, "I wonder if many males are not a bit less sure of their maleness and masculinity than females of their femaleness and femininity; the greater amount of homosexual hallucinations and delusions reported in male paranoid psychotics might point to this."

He adds, "Perhaps this is evidence that the core gender identity is more endangered in males than females. Females do not need, and males are unable at first, to escape from having to identify with a female (mother) from birth on."

He also points out that parents who are happy to have a daughter help create and foster her femininity. She does not question why she was born female, nor does she possess the strong wish she had been a boy. She easily embarks on "an essential beginning of femininity and sexuality."

For both men and women who wish to have a fulfilling sexual and marital life, it is important that if they feel in any way troubled, either before or after marriage, they look at the feelings that lie behind their inevitable anger and depression.

For if we cannot examine our own reasons for feeling unhappy we are apt not to feel any happier later in life no matter who we choose as marital partner. It does little good to blame someone else for the troubled conflicts that lie within us—that have stirred within us from far earlier days in life.

8 🐑 When Rage Leads to Murder and Suicide

Most murders and suicides are caused in large part by an explosive childhood rage buried since earlier days when the original anger was felt toward the mother or father who, in some way, brought deep fear into the child's life.

The fear could be of abandonment or violence or sexual abuse or inordinate neglect inflicted on the child. Or the child witnessed violence in the house between his or her parents. There is also the fear, which may be exaggerated, of the loss of love of a parent when siblings are present and excessive jealousy causes a deep rage.

In later life the threat of or actual abandonment of one marital partner by the other may lead to murder or suicide. *The New York Post* reported on January 20, 1989, that James Reid, forty-one years old, a Brooklyn school-bus driver, despondent after his wife, a nurse, left him, and took their two young sons, shot to death his teenage daughter who stayed with him because she loved him, then turned the gun on himself.

Police refused to tell reporters whether the wife, Judith, had complained about family violence. But several neighbors claimed that two weeks before, Reid beat his wife so severely she required stitches to her head. She dropped charges against her husband and fled to Florida with her sons, neighbors said.

That same day *The New York Times* carried a full report on Patrick Edward Purdy, who lived in Stockton, California, and who, three days earlier, had gone on a bloody rampage at the Cleveland Elementary School. He murdered five Southeast Asian children and wounded thirty others, most of them Vietnamese and Cambodian. He then committed suicide with the AK-47 assault rifle.

He was only twenty-four years old and police told reporters Purdy was "a troubled loner full of hate who could not keep a job and had alcohol and drug problems." Interviews with family members and coworkers at the various places that hired him showed he disliked everybody, but particularly authority figures such as police officers. Captain Dennis Perry, of the Stockton Police Department, told reporters, "Throughout

101

his lifetime, Mr. Purdy developed a hate for everybody. He had no friends, no particular girlfriends."

Captain Perry also noted that Purdy had tried to hang himself in 1988 when jailed for firing a weapon in the Tahoe Basin, saying, "He had a lot of family problems. It was a split family with different step-mothers and stepfathers. His real father was killed in an auto accident in 1981. And his mother is an alcoholic."

Even from this sparse information we might guess that Purdy's child-hood was one that built up deep rage within against siblings. He felt a titanic anger he was unable to hide from the world as he roamed from one place to another until it exploded and caused the death of five in-nocent youngsters and his own.

Few murders have aroused such horror as that committed by lawyer Joel Steinberg, who killed his six-year-old adopted daughter Lisa. His mother appeared briefly one night on television a few months before his conviction to insist that he was a "very good son." She was dressed in a plain frock, low-heeled shoes and looked as though she might be his grandmother.

We know from Hedda Nussbaum, who lived with him, and from oth-ers that he was a violent, cruel man, often broke the law when it came to arranging homes for adoptive children. He introduced Hedda to free-basing cocaine.

An interesting article appeared in *People*, February 13, 1989, written by a former Hunter College classmate of Hedda's, Naomi Weiss, with Bonnie Johnson. The article reveals how Hedda first became attracted to Steinberg and why she stayed with him. Hedda allowed herself to be emotionally and physically abused by Steinberg. Ms. Weiss wrote that the last time she saw Hedda before the news of Lisa's death broke in the newspapers was at a shower in 1981 celebrating Lisa's arrival in the Steinberg apartment, where friends and family celebrated the occasion. Ms. Weiss and Hedda talked on the phone frequently in the months that followed but eventually drifted apart. Then, as Ms. Weiss put it, on her way to work November 3, 1987, she spotted Hedda, "black and blue and swollen," on the front page of every New York newspaper. She read with disbelief the details of Lisa's short stay in the hospital, gravely injured, apparently dying and of Hedda's physical condition: her nose splayed, her upper lip cleft, sixteen ribs broken and a leg so badly lacer-ated that doctors considered amputation.

"It seemed impossible," Ms. Weiss wrote, that "this was the caring, loving friend I had studied and double-dated with, the friend who scribbled comments with me about our sexy male teachers in our notebooks, the tall, elegant, dark-haired beauty who came to my wedding in 1965, shortly after our graduation from college."

Encouraged by her second husband, Ms. Weiss, after several months, made her first trip to Four Winds, the private psychiatric hospital in Katonah, New York, where Hedda was being treated. Hedda was "unrecognizable." Mrs. Weiss said she wanted "to run away, to cry alone at what Steinberg had done to her."

As they talked, Ms. Weiss said she felt as though she were with a stranger; "it was as if Hedda had been locked away in a cave for the past five years."

According to Dr. Samuel Klagsbrun, director of Four Winds, who treated Hedda personally and without charge, her low self-esteem as a child and adult made her particularly vulnerable to a controlling and domineering man like Steinberg. Because of her background she needed emotional security at any price, Dr. Klagsbrun added.

Ms. Weiss's article reveals how fear of abandonment in a child can cause a later willingness as an adult to endure violence, even at the cost of a life itself, in order to avoid being alone in the world. Ms. Weiss recalled that Hedda once told her that when Hedda was two, she became very attached to her grandmother, who lived in the home along with Hedda's mother, Emma, and Hedda's father, William, a retired hairdresser, and Hedda's sister Judy, older by twenty-two months.

Hedda then recalled that her grandmother soon suffered a nervous breakdown and was hospitalized. Hedda said to Judy, "I didn't understand. I thought I must have done something to make her leave me. When she came home a few months later, she stayed in her room with the door shut. I hardly ever had real emotional contact with her again. She lived with us like that until her death twenty years later and I lived with that rejection every single day."

She later lived with Steinberg's rejection "every single day" and most nights. Perhaps unconsciously she was still trying to win back the love he first showed. As her grandmother had shown love at first, then what Hedda, in her primitive child-mind thought was hate as the grandmother retired from everyone to live alone in her room. We always repeat the past of early life when it comes to a traumatic event, such as abandonment by a loved one. We might guess that Hedda feared abandonment more than death itself. She was willing to take the beatings of a Steinberg in the hope of again earning his love, rather than be tossed out alone into the unfriendly world.

Hedda told Ms. Weiss, "I was always trying to be a good girl so I wouldn't be left alone. I was very shy and timid. And I never showed any anger." Nor did she in her life with Steinberg, as she later related in court. She was the docile, beaten mistress, who would never lift her voice in protest no matter how severely he hurt her, physically and mentally. She would never disobey him even if it meant a little girl might die. She wanted never to lose him, to suffer life alone, a far worse fate than the beatings. The neglected little child was still strong in Hedda—it was no coincidence she became a children's book editor.

Another early factor in Hedda's dependency was that her mother fostered an "intense bonding" in the two sisters, Ms. Weiss reports. Mrs. Nussbaum dressed the two girls alike and they had the same friends, Judy's friends. "It was always 'we' or 'us,' never 'I' or 'me,'" says Ms. Weiss. "As a result, Hedda thinks, she never really developed a sense of herself."

For Hedda, the beatings became "a way of life" with Steinberg, Ms. Weiss wrote. "Even in 1981, after a series of blows required her to undergo surgery for a ruptured spleen, Hedda says, 'I didn't see myself as being battered. To me, the beatings were isolated incidents. I always thought each one was the last. I loved Joel so much. I felt there was much more good between us than not.'"

Hedda provided the prosecution with a list of more than thirty physical domestic cruelties, though there were many more—in court she was only allowed to speak of five. According to Ms. Weiss, Steinberg, "a versatile attacker, had kicked her in the eye, strangled her, beaten her sexual organs, urinated on her, hung her in handcuffs from a chinning bar, lacerated a tear duct by poking his finger in the corner of her eye, broken her nose several times and pulled out clumps of hair while throwing her about their apartment. He also would take the blowtorch they used for freebasing cocaine and move it near to her skin so that she would have burn marks all over her body."

In 1978 Hedda accepted a snort of cocaine from one of Joel's clients. She told Ms. Weiss, "It was fun. I was always the good girl trying to do all the right things, and this made me feel naughty." But from the end of that year through the middle of 1984 Hedda ran away six times, seeking refuge with friends, in hospitals or in a women's shelter. In the end she always returned to Steinberg because she missed Lisa, or was lured back by a display of overwhelming affection from Joel, or because she did not want him to worry. Ms. Weiss remarks, "Not once did any of the people or agencies she turned to recognize the urgency of her cries for help."

Dr. Klagsbrun told Ms. Weiss that it was very unlikely these attempts by Hedda to free herself could have succeeded because Joel "had become so incorporated into Hedda's system that she couldn't see herself not under his control. Separation from him would mean that she would perish."

Ms. Weiss concludes her article by saying Hedda learned a lot about herself during her stay at Four Winds and perhaps her most difficult accomplishment "was learning to get angry." Hedda told her, "That was a big step for me. I also learned to see Joel clearly. He lied to me, and he robbed me of my two children, my motherhood and my career. I'm angry at him for that."

Early in her therapy, Four Winds asked her to keep a visual notebook of her feelings and she drew herself as frightened—"hearing no evil, seeing no evil and speaking no evil." She told Ms. Weiss just before Steinberg's trial, "I hear, I see and I'm ready to speak."

Her therapy, as Ms. Weiss says, will help her deal with a whole range of new fears—getting a job, living independently and dealing with a world that can sometimes be hostile. Hedda will have to face her devastating fear of being alone, of living with the childhood fear of abandonment, which means death to a child. She had to live through a child's imagined death to receive the emotional help she drastically needed. Somehow her parents failed to give the strengths, the love needed, for her to slowly gain the courage to mature psychologically.

As to what caused Steinberg's cruelty, we can only assume it stemmed from childhood experiences with his mother and father. As an only child he would receive the full brunt of their love and hate. Perhaps one day he will honestly describe the traumatic scenes he recalls from his early life so we can understand more completely the suffering that led to such brutality and murder.

A front-page story in *The New York Times* of March 22, 1989, written by Fox Butterfield, described the horror in the life of Willie Bosket, a self-proclaimed "monster" whose five-year sentence at the age of fifteen for two subway murders led New York to strengthen its juvenile criminal law. He was now being sentenced for his latest crime at twenty-six, stabbing a prison guard.

He once admitted he committed more than two thousand crimes between the ages of nine and fifteen, including twenty-five stabbings. He is serving a sentence of twenty-eight years to life for assault and arson. Considered the most violent inmate in New York State, he is confined to a specially designed cell stripped of everything including lighting fixtures, to prevent him from swallowing them, as he tried in the past.

Raised on West 145th Street in Harlem, he never met his father who had a similar life of crime. Willie's mother and grandmother would say to him, "He's a bad man and you're just like him." His mother works as a security guard, carries a gun.

He was uncontrollable from third grade on, started then to stab people. Asked how he felt after shooting and killing two people, he told police, "I shot people, that's all. I don't feel nothing."

His mother was pregnant with Willie when his father was arrested for a double murder at twenty. His father later escaped prison, robbed a bank and made the FBI's most-wanted list before being caught and sentenced to the federal penitentiary at Leavenworth, Kansas. He finally killed himself and a girlfriend when caught in a police shoot-out in 1983 as he tried to escape from prison.

There is no more certain way to mold a little boy into a "monster" than to bring him up, as Willie's mother did, reminding him that his father was "a bad man and you're just like him." A little boy's model is his father, he tries to be just like him, unconsciously and consciously copying his father. In this case Willie was perhaps also avoiding femininity; he did not want to be "a security guard," protecting others against "bad" people, the way his mother did. Instead of getting help from a child guidance agency when Willie first started attacking innocent bystanders, his mother asked police to send him away to an institution. This could only make her son even more violent and determined on revenge.

When parents are cruel to children and to each other, cannot provide love and security, a child's primitive passions become intensified. The child may later carry out the violent wishes of his earliest role models.

The study of a fourteen-year-old girl who murdered her father showed she had fulfilled the wishes of her mother, who openly hated her husband and had wished him dead for years. The girl's hatred of her father, a brutal man who beat her and her mother, finally flamed into a murderous rage, fanned by her mother's hatred of him.

What makes the difference between someone who merely fantasizes murder and someone who actually kills? Studies suggest that the degree of violence, actual and threatened, experienced by a child at the hands

or voice or threatening looks of his mother or father makes the difference. If a child feels fairly at ease in the family, his normal fantasies
of revenge are easily handled and sublimated, need no outlet. But when
he continually feels his life is emotionally or actually at stake, murderous fantasies may one day overpower his conscious control.

A number of psychoanalysts have written of the effect of the unconscious, unspoken, criminal wishes of parents on the behavior of children. They have pointed out that in the legend of Oedipus, the tragic
act was originally set in motion by his parents. They ordered the infant
Oedipus murdered by a shepherd to prevent the prophecy of the Del-
phic oracle from coming true—that he would grow up to kill his father
and marry his mother.

There is evidence that if a mother encourages her child to express
violence and rage, the child may later turn to violent acts, having her
tacit approval to do so. Whereas if she punishes the child for expressing
an anger that is intense, the child turns inward his murderous feelings
toward her and may become schizophrenic. Excessive guilt over angry
feelings may induce mental illness, a form of self-punishment, whereas
lack of guilt over angry feelings and permission to express them may
lead to violent behavior.

Fantasies of childhood revenge underlie every murder. In his unconscious, the adult murderer takes revenge on the cruel mother and father
of childhood, no matter who the victim. Sometimes the victim *is* the
original target of hatred, as in the case of Lizzie Borden of Fall
River, Massachusetts, who murdered her father and his new wife in
1892—reversal in sex of the Oedipus complex where a son kills his father and marries his mother.

This cause of murder has fascinated mankind over the centuries as
has the Electra complex. This complex was named after the daughter
of Agamemnon and Clytemnestra, who persuaded her brother Orestes
to kill their mother and her lover who had murdered Agamemnon.

Since the aggressive drive goes through developmental stages, in Lizzie Borden's life there was in childhood earlier feelings of deep anger
when her mother was alive. We can surmise the relationship between
Lizzie and her mother was not a very loving one as Lizzie competed for
her father's love.

Then, on the later oedipal level, it seems evident she had never overcome her passionate attachment to her father. She considered him her
possession, especially after her mother died. He colluded in this fantasy
by giving her his wedding ring, as though he symbolically now selected

her as his bride. When he remarried, Lizzie's feelings of rejection, betrayal and jealousy must have been overwhelming. She managed to conceal her fury until one hot summer day when it erupted in a rampage that culminated in the murder of her father and her rival stepmother. The murders may also have taken place at this particular time because her father was about to change his will and leave most of his estate to his second wife, cutting Lizzie out of his life even further.

The deep hatred between siblings that leads to murder is another recurrent theme in ancient myths. The biblical story of Cain and Abel is the most famous example. And if ever Freud's point needed to be proved—that in the unconscious part of the mind every murderer is killing one or all members of his childhood family—the case of Richard Speck did so. In Chicago on a July day in 1966, Speck murdered eight student nurses. There were eight persons in his childhood he must have hated—two brothers, four sisters, his mother and stepfather. The eight nurses symbolically represented the slaughter of Speck's family.

It is no coincidence that most murders occur when someone who is loved (loved-hated) threatens abandonment or actually leaves. Authorities estimate that over 70 percent of murders are committed against someone supposedly "near and dear," often when the victim threatens to walk out. In Chicago in 1965, out of 395 persons murdered, 31 were husbands killed by wives and 45 were wives killed by husbands. Only 7 were gangland murders in this city once reigned over by Al Capone.

Psychoanalysts believe that a baby's first fear is that if his mother abandons him he will be annihilated—will die of starvation. A baby cannot survive without the care of a mother or a substitute figure. This fear of abandonment related to an early painful experience may persist into later life, transferred on someone who is close. The need for this mothering figure in some women may be so acute they prefer that the one who plans to abandon them die—so that no one else can possess him.

Many men believe women still have to be "conquered" like an enemy but also idealize them, like a distant goddess—the child's split fantasies. When the idealization proves false, as it always does, for no human can be a god, the men curse, berate, sometimes even kill the woman they believe deceived and failed them. The concept that the mother be "perfect" is the demand of every child. To become mature means giving up this unrealistic expectation.

A number of women who have felt abandoned by the men they love, unable to tolerate the thought of killing anyone, turn the wish to kill on themselves. In their suicide notes they often state they hope the survivor who abandoned them will suffer as they suffered. Several prominent Hollywood movie actresses over the years, abandoned by famous actors, have left such tragic notes.

Not only women but many men have committed suicide. And siblings have murdered each other. In March 1989 a Brooklyn teenager was charged with killing her older half sister by throwing a firebomb into their bedroom. They had argued, then the younger woman filled a bottle with gasoline, lit it and hurled it through a window of the apartment.

Firefighters, responding to the 12:20 P.M. blaze, fought through the intense smoke and flames and pulled the older sister from the apartment. But she was pronounced dead on the sidewalk by a fire department spokesman. Her younger sister was charged with murder and arson.

Violence has become far more pervasive in our society as the use of drugs has increased to alarming proportions and the rate of murder risen in all cities. In his book *Violent Deaths in the United States: An Epidemiologic Study of Suicide, Homicide and Accidents*, Dr. Paul C. Holinger discusses the need to understand man's "self-destructiveness." He claims it is possible to predict patterns of violent deaths that emerge from psychological reasons and urges "preventive strategies to reduce violent deaths."

Children who have been abused or neglected by parents often play with matches and "accidently" set the family's apartment on fire as a way of crying out for help. Frank Bruni, a reporter for *The New York Post*, wrote on February 21, 1989, that New York City fire investigator Charles Wagner suspected this and set out to question children who had set fires about family abuse.

A seven-year-old girl playing with matches that set her family's apartment on fire told him she was a victim of abuse. She said her sister often beat her with a belt and her father sometimes slapped her so hard she could see his handprint on her face in the mirror.

Wagner reported a growing number of children "reached out for help" in this way, starting fires "to signal they've been abused." Wagner is coordinator of the Fire Department's Juvenile Firesetters Intervention Program, which he started in 1986 to study children who caused fires. He reported that his findings revealed more than half the children under fourteen who played with fire are not "just making mischief."

"They are crying out for help," Wagner said. "And if we don't recognize that and get them counseling or assistance, they're likely to do it again."

He studied 125 children under fourteen who started fires in the Bronx between November 1986 and November 1987. He discovered that seventy-three felt enough anger or stress in their lives to need at least some initial psychological counseling and they were referred to the city's Department of Mental Health. Twelve of the children lived in such horrifying circumstances, Wagner said, that they had to be placed with child welfare agencies.

Psychiatrists are not surprised that children set fires as a way of asking for help. Dr. Reed Moscowitz of the New York University Medical Center explained that starting fires is one of the early ways when children are young "to act out their anger and frustration, even if it's not a conscious act."

Bruni in his *Post* article quoted Jean Pratt, assistant city commissioner of mental health in the Bronx, as saying that many children referred to her by Wagner's program have parents who are drug addicts. She told Bruni, "One kid's mother was renting out the little girl's bedroom to prostitutes so she could afford to buy crack. The little girl burned the bedroom down."

Wagner said that discovering the underlying reasons children start fires is crucial to fire prevention, since many juvenile fire starters will act again. Some experts estimate that in urban areas, children under eighteen are responsible for half of all incendiary fires that claim thousands of American lives every year.

In spite of the drug craze, if it can be controlled by our authorities, we may see murder decline as more angry, unhappy men and women (mostly men, for they commit the largest number of murders by far) can face the rage within themselves. Rage that started in childhood in a home where they felt they were unwanted, cruelly treated, outcast. They tell of their wish for revenge in the act of murder, which spells out their vengeance on inhumane parents of earlier days. As studies are made on the earlier lives of murderers, it becomes apparent the wish to murder started in their hearts as children.

The rage that exists in the multiple personality is a devastating one, according to Emily Peterson, coauthor of *Nightmare*. This is an account of how she helped save the life of a fifteen-year-old girl in her English literature class in a high school in Ontario, California. The girl, Nancy Lynn Gooch, was helped by Emily over a period of twelve years to face the terror and anger she had suffered ever since she was sexually molested as a little girl, both by her grandmother and a young man who lived nearby.

The buried fury Nancy had never dared express, an appropriate rage judging by what she had suffered mentally and physically from the early attacks, became so powerful and overwhelming she had dared not display any of it to anyone, especially since she had been threatened by her assailants that she and her parents would die if she spoke of what had happened.

Ms. Peterson explains that the fantasy in such a case remains that the anger could destroy the world if it were expressed in any way. It felt to Nancy that if she ever released any of the anger, the person against whom it was directed would die. At first, the anger was not always a conscious feeling. During Nancy's treatment she started to become aware of it, acted it out against Ms. Peterson during her treatment sessions as she gained trust in her therapist.

The average person as a rule represses far less anger than the multiple personality, Ms. Peterson explains, for he does not suffer to the degree the attacked multiple personality does. But, she says, "It is important if you feel deeply unhappy to realize and admit that anger underlies the unhappiness and then have the courage to accept the anger. You can then control it rather than have it control you."

She points out we are all taught as children not to show how angry we feel. As we grow up we learn it is our "fault" if we in any way antagonize our parents. She says, "If my mother broke a dish or burned a stew, she would turn to me and say, 'Look what you made me do!' She blamed me, her child, as the cause of her own mistakes. Parents do this all the time.

"This made me angry, even at the age of six, because part of me knew it was not my fault," she concludes. "But the part of me that accepted my mother as the authority in my life believed her. And the anger within, intensified by my acceptance of her words, had to be repressed even more deeply, time after time, as I was blamed."

Most of us do not become murderers, our anger is not as intense as; that of the one who kills out of a rage that cannot be controlled. To commit murder is to show the ultimate in hatred not only of the victim but of the self.

9 🔊 How Rage Affects Our Body

There seems no doubt that rage has a powerful capacity to produce internal changes of a bodily nature if someone hurts us emotionally or physically. For we become automatically consumed by an anger we may or may not suppress. If we hide it from ourselves we may suffer psychosomatic disorders that reflect our strong emotions composed of fear, rage and guilt.

Socrates once told the physicians of Greece they were not effective because they did not know that the body could not be cured without taking the mind into consideration. About this same time in history, 400 BC, Hippocrates, the father of medicine, maintained, "In order to cure the human body, it is necessary to have a knowledge of the whole of things." He meant what was going on in the patient's mind.

Referring to more recent views, a headline in *The New York Post* of January 17, 1989, stated, "Losing Temper May Lose You Your Life." There followed the story of how high levels of hostility and anger when dealing with others take a high toll on the body, according to Dr. Redford Williams, Jr., of Duke University Medical Center, as he addressed a meeting of the American Heart Association in Monterey, California.

Though intellectually we may try to keep body and mind separate, emotionally we cannot, any more than we can stop our heart from beating or our lungs from breathing. Our buried-from-awareness emotions are the cause of most physical distress. There is no organ of the body, no system of the body, that may not be affected by our subterranean thoughts and wishes. The ills accompanying mental anguish are found literally from head to toe and from the inner lining of the intestinal tract to the outer layer of skin covering us.

When we allow ourselves to become fatigued and vulnerable to illness we are showing a sign of emotional distress. Tension, depression, mourning, loss of a loved one, fear of sexual desire, or of hostile impulses, all may become converted into illness in any part of the body. Physical illness in a sense is often the way our body tries to help out when we feel overburdened with mental conflicts.

When we fall physically ill we may be telling of concealed wishes, including the wish to be cared for and loved, the wish to retreat from the world of reality temporarily, the wish to express feelings we dare not consciously admit.

Freud discovered a new way of thinking about physical, as well as psychic, illness. He proved that our emotions could cause physical illness. That a paralyzed arm could be the result of a "paralyzed" emotion. That a headache could reflect the wish not to think about something believed dangerous to our self-esteem. That blindness could represent the wish not to see something we believed obscene and evil.

Psychoanalysts call the illness, whether it be earache, stomachache, headache or ulcer, a "symptom." The symptom is the surface eruption of the buried feelings that cause inner distress and seek some outlet. The symptom is one way of discharging some of the anxiety aroused by hidden, forbidden feelings tied to a wish we deem "bad" or "wrong."

A symptom may reflect not only reality but fantasy. If you imagine you are being poisoned, this may cause the same reaction in your body as though you *were* poisoned. There have been instances in which a man bitten by a snake he believes poisonous dies, but from a heart attack caused by fear, not by the nonexistent poison.

No one has to take the word of Freud and other psychoanalysts that emotions may cause bodily illness. A famous nonpsychoanalyst, Dr. Walter B. Cannon, showed that the direct expression of psychological states could produce physical symptoms.

He proved through tests on men and women that emotions—particularly rage—caused profound changes in our body chemistry. These changes were principally due to the production of sugar by the activity of the adrenal glands. Disturbances also occurred in the respiratory and circulatory systems and gastrointestinal tract. Cannon measured changing units of hydrochloric acid secreted by the stomach, variations in blood pressure shown in the mercury columns of blood-pressure machines, and disturbances in the rhythm of the heartbeat as pictured by the electrocardiogram.

He substantiated his belief that when a flood of anxiety pours into the brain's higher cortical centers—those that control our conscious thinking—the anxiety may paralyze these centers. Then the subcortical centers, our autonomic nervous system, go into action as kind of a substitute director. However, our autonomic nervous system reacts in a rigid pattern because it is not subject to our "will" but is automatic. It is governed by our primary thinking system, which means it gives symbolic, rather than direct expression as outlet for the repressed emotions our conscious has been unable to handle.

The changes that take place form emotional stress independently of what we call "willpower." The body's reaction to "fight or flight" from a dangerous situation occurs whether the emotion causing the changes is conscious or unconscious.

Cannon thus called attention to a "too common unwillingness among physicians to regard seriously the emotional elements in disease," as he put it. His classic book, *Bodily Changes in Pain, Hunger, Fear, and Rage*, published in 1929, described his research into the relationship of feelings and changes within the body.

An employer speaks harshly to his secretary, calls her "stupid" because she has typed one word incorrectly, not taking into consideration that everyone is entitled to an error or two. The secretary feels like hitting back at her boss, both physically (always our first reaction, our most primitive feeling) and verbally. But she bites her tongue, says not a word, wishing to keep her job. She represses all outward expression of her emotion, but this does not mean it has disappeared. Its effect is now channeled to various parts of her body. Her heartbeat may accelerate. She may feel like vomiting. Or the blood sugar in her body may rise.

Thus an emotion of rage, if suppressed, does not disappear but finds substitute, partial gratification in some other part of the body. This means that, dismissed by our conscious, or cortical, control, the emotion falls under the domination of the thalamus. The thalamus controls the unconscious part of our mind.

This explains why, in many instances, psychoanalysts know it is of little use to try to argue a patient out of his or her emotional reactions since the cortex, or his or her reason, has little direct control over the unconscious thoughts that dominate so much of behavior. Those hidden feelings that are the source of conflict must be brought to the patient's awareness. Physical symptoms disappear as the unconscious conflicts that caused them become conscious.

A man of twenty-nine, who worked on the New York Stock Exchange, suffered severe asthma for two years and went into analysis, after doctors told him they could find no physical cause. Three months into analysis one day as he lay on the couch, tears suddenly started to trickle down his face as he recalled, "My heart was broken when I was five and my mother took my older brother to a movie but left me home, saying I was too young to go. I knew she loved him more than she loved me. I don't think I ever forgave her."

He pulled out his handkerchief, wiped the tears away. Then he said, in amazement, "My asthma seems to have disappeared. How could that be?"

The analyst said, "Men are not supposed to cry when they feel hurt or angry. But parts of the body may suffer, in a sense crying for them. If you can cry, you won't need your asthma to tell of your suffering."

The classic paper on the psychological interpretation of asthma and other respiratory illnesses was written in 1931 by Dr. Otto Fenichel, called "Respiratory Introjection." The concept of respiratory introjection was first described by Freud in 1918 in his case study "From the History of an Infantile Neurosis."

This was the story of the Wolf Man, as he became known, because of his persistent dream of several white wolves sitting motionless in a tree outside his window at night. This dream led Freud to important insights about the effect on a baby of seeing or hearing a mother and father in the act of sex. The Wolf Man was possessed by phobias, including one that affected his breathing. Whenever he saw beggars, cripples or very old men on the street, he felt compelled to exhale forcibly "so as not to become like them." Under certain conditions (Freud did not describe what these were but they may have related to the man's sexual activities) he "had to draw in his breath vigorously."

This meant, Freud said, the Wolf Man was unconsciously inhaling, then exhaling, the image of the beggar, cripple or old man. Freud related this to the heavy breathing the man had heard from his father during sexual intercourse when, as an infant, he had slept in his parents' bedroom. Psychoanalysts advise parents to give the infant a room of his own from the day he is born.

Fenichel was the first to write in detail of the importance of respiratory introjection—the childhood fantasy that you "take in" through your nose the image of someone as a way of keeping him close. Freud called this "incorporation of the lost object." Via the fantasy of incorporating what he believes is the lost mother, a baby consoles himself by thinking, "My loved one is not gone, I now carry it within myself and I can never lose it." This was the thought of Dr. Karl Abraham, psychoanalyst, who studied the early psychic stages of the infant and how it affected later behavior. The "loved object" is the image of the mother as she feeds him, either by breast or bottle.

Elaborating on Freud's theory, Fenichel emphasized the erotic qualities of respiratory introjection. He maintained the mother of infancy is seen by the baby as giving both protection and "satisfaction in the erotic aspects of feeding." This "protective sexual satisfaction is unconsciously perceived as the aim of respiratory introjection." In other words, breathing in the image of the mother is sensed by a baby primarily as an erotic act.

Primitive people, psychotics and children believe they can breathe in substances from the outer world and return substances to it. The substance "is invisible and therefore suitable for conveying magical ideas, which is reflected in the equation of life and soul with breathing, which further lends itself to magical use because it is the one vegetative function that can be regulated and influenced voluntarily," Fenichel explained.

We may regulate our breathing to imitate someone else's rhythm, thus trying to become one with him, as tap dancers or chorus girls onstage try to become as one when they dance in unison. Inhaling the same air as another person carries the implication of being united with him whereas exhalation means separation.

Psychoanalysts also point out that someone who has asthma may be displaying a conflict caused by angry feelings as a child at the mother, now appearing in converted form as the symptom of asthma. The sufferer has transferred his earlier furious feelings, now barred from awareness, to his bodily ailment.

Our breathing processes lie at the very root of anxiety and rage. When we become upset, we are apt to breathe more heavily. When we are frightened, as in a dentist's office or hospital, we may have difficulty breathing. This is due, according to psychoanalysts, to the existence of an unconscious preparedness for anxiety situations.

The wheezing, gasping and rhythmic noises of the asthmatic may be connected to any scene or scenes that frightened the infant, violent or sexual, psychoanalysts say. Dr. Anita Stevens, a psychiatrist in New York, author of *Your Mind Can Cure*, describes a young woman in her late twenties who came to her suffering from asthma. She had been plagued by attacks since the age of eight. Antiallergenic medications did not seem to help.

After a few weeks the patient told Dr. Stevens, "I have always been very jealous of my younger and prettier sister. I know my mother and father loved her more than they did me. They would often criticize me but never her."

Then, amid wheezes and the catching of her breath, she described an evening when she was eight and her sister six. She recalled, "We were having a pillow fight on our beds, we slept in the same room in twin beds. Suddenly Mary placed her pillow over my mouth and pressed hard, as if she were trying to smother me. At first I laughed, thinking it was a game. Then I couldn't catch my breath. I felt I was suffocating. I couldn't even get breath enough to scream."

She stopped for a moment, then went on, "I thought I was going to die. But somehow I managed to pull free. I tore myself away from the pillow. I wanted to kill Mary. To suffocate *her* as she tried to do me. But all I could do was stare at her in horror. And later, when my mother came in to kiss us good night, I didn't even tell her what Mary had done."

Then she turned to Dr. Stevens, asked piteously, "Wasn't that an awful thing for a sister to do?"

"It certainly was," Dr. Stevens agreed. "You must have been filled with rage."

"I guess so," the woman said. "Since I remember I felt like killing her."

"Mary tried to suffocate you when you were eight and that's the very age you started to get asthma attacks," Dr. Stevens said. "Do you see a connection?"

"Like I was suffocating myself to death?" she asked.

"Like you were doing to yourself what you wanted to do to her. An eye for an eye, in revenge. A wish about which you felt very guilty. You couldn't even tell your mother what your sister had done. You suffered in silence. But your desire to get even was a deep one. Not only because you felt she had tried to kill you but, as you said earlier, because you thought your parents loved her more."

The woman started to cry. She cried on and off at her sessions for the next few weeks as she talked more of her buried feelings about her younger sister, mother and father, exorcising her hatred and envy. Her asthma slowly disappeared, she found she could breathe normally.

Other illnesses of the respiratory system are often amenable to such treatment. Illnesses that affect this system, we might say, show among other things an unconscious wish to "breathe in" something believed taboo (the heavy breathing of those in a rage) and then "breathe it out" with a vengeance, as it were.

It has also been shown that our violent fantasies may lie hidden in phobias that defend against both destructive and sexual wishes. A phobia is the reaction to the threat of an inner wish regarded as dangerous to the self. A man who washes his hands continuously during the day may be afraid of "dirty" thoughts, such as the wish to masturbate or to have an affair with someone who is married.

The body is not just the sum of its parts. Psychic processes are involved in its movements, giving a certain unknown quality to the way we act and think. These mental processes are governed by what Freud called "the principle of constancy." Our psychic processes strive to maintain an equilibrium in the mind so it may be free for our conscious thoughts, needed to carry us through the day.

Thoughts never vanish, no thought is ever lost to the unconscious, which stores it forever. If something we wished to do, such as in the previous anecdote the older sister had wished to "kill" her younger sister for trying to suffocate her, is blocked, the wish may continue to be expressed through bodily symptoms.

Our life is governed by our wishes, both conscious and unconscious. The wish comes first, then the mind decides what to do about it— whether to act on it or reject it. We cannot move without the wish propelling our body into action. A wish may upset what Freud called the "constancy" of the mind. Like a storm-driven wind stirring a field of wheat, the wish may arouse tension in the mind. This tension must be resolved, either in carrying out the wish or distributing the psychic energy elsewhere, so equilibrium may be restored to the conscious mind. Unless the tension is eased, the psyche will be overwhelmed by stimuli from within and without and cannot function normally, which is what happens in psychosis.

In the interest of bodily survival, our mind is usually prepared to combat outer danger, such as fleeing a threatening assassin or a car speeding toward us, out of control. But the dangers within us are not as easy to flee as we bury them from consciousness, only to feel their power in physical illnesses that may eventually cripple us.

During analysis, as patients make conscious those unconscious wishes thought dangerous, they then "suppress" the wish, which is a conscious act, rather than "repress" it, which they have done unconsciously. It is the *denial* of the wish, the lack of awareness of what we feel—most often our violent wishes and our sexual wishes—that does us in psychologically.

Psychoanalysts have discovered that one of the fantasies in "overeating" is the wish to destroy, by eating, someone who has caused buried

rage. One woman became aware that each time she felt furious at a relative or friend, she would rush to the refrigerator for something to de-
vour. When she felt at peace with herself, she noticed she was never
so voracious.

Life would be easy if there were not the complication of a conflict
between the id on one side and the ego and superego on the other. For,
what our id craves often lies in direct opposition to what our superego
(or conscience) dictates. Our instincts may drive us to a deeply desired
pleasure but society allows us only limited pleasure. Thus there will be
emotional warfare at times within ourselves.

When we deny direct gratification to a feeling like rage it must somehow find a partial outlet. We cannot bottle it up, throw it away. It tries
to escape in various ways, some of which we may have trouble han-
dling. If the wish finds an approved form of expression, we feel our self-
respect rise. But if the wish is used to create symptoms of physical or
emotional pain, we will suffer.

One psychiatrist told of a husband who complained of severe arthritis
in his right arm. Nothing seemed to ease the pain. Finally, he went to
a hypnotist who placed him in a trance, told him he must give up the
illness, assured him that when he returned home, his arm would feel
normal. The next morning when the man awoke there was no pain in
his arm. He got out of bed, went to the kitchen, grabbed a knife and
stabbed his wife to death.

He confessed to the psychiatrist, when the latter visited him in
prison, that for years he had held back an overwhelming hatred for his
wife, often wishing she were dead so he would be free of her. He had
unconsciously paralyzed the arm with which he wished to murder her,
to prevent his body from attempting to come to the rescue of his desperate rage at his inability to free himself from his wife. But when the
physical restraint he imposed on himself was suddenly removed, he was
unable to control his violent, primitive wish to kill her and gain his
freedom.

This is an extreme example of how the body may try to come to the
rescue of a mind unconsciously consumed by rage. But it shows, according to Freud's theories, the protective purpose physical symptoms may
try to serve and the danger of removing them suddenly without understanding their deeper causes.

Psychoanalysts have been successful in easing physical ailments
caused by emotional conflicts, known as "psychosomatic illnesses." The

physical pains—headaches, sinus, constant colds, ulcers, colitis, among others—are often among the earliest symptoms to disappear shortly after the patient starts treatment.

The relationship between emotional pain and asthma was made clear in *One Little Boy*, written by Dorothy Baruch in 1952. Dr. Baruch, with her husband, Dr. Hyman Miller, a child psychologist and author, showed how the asthma attacks a seven-year-old boy suffered since the age of three disappeared after he went into therapy. The boy, Kenneth, had also been failing in school but as a result of Dr. Baruch's help became one of the top pupils in his class.

The book also reported the treatment of a family, for his parents undertook group therapy. This helped them look at their problems more realistically and indirectly helped their young son.

Dr. Baruch graphically described the way in which the emotional conflicts of a mother and father may affect a child, for children react with great sensitivity to everything in the atmosphere—the unspoken as well as the spoken. As she put it, "Feelings and thoughts are not absent because they are not spoken. *Not-heard* does not mean *not-present*. . . . A child may sense his parents' unconscious feelings."

She also emphasized that every child takes both little and big occurrences from the world that surrounds him and weaves fantasies that may be strange and primitive. He may also misinterpret his parents' feelings and acts. He may imagine he is more wronged, more threatened, less loved than he actually is. Then the resentment, anxiety, fear and guilt that color his fantasies loom out of all proportion and his emotions hold great terror.

The same basic thoughts and feelings in one child may cause conflicts that result in asthma or failure in school, whereas in another child they produce problems of discipline, conflicts with other children or teachers. In a third child, the same basic thoughts and feelings cause no problems because he has felt loved, has been treated with respect, not sarcasm or scorn, or ignored. We all possess the same instinctual drives and needs with which to cope. It depends on whether we feel wanted or unwanted by parents as to how we react to the drives and needs—whether violently or with comparative ease.

As Kenneth could express his anger in play, his asthma disappeared. His anger "was draining out through the drama of killing, it did not need for the moment to drain out in asthma," as Dr. Baruch put it. She believed that if Kenneth no longer denied his aggressive feelings, the energy he used to hold them from awareness would be freed for work and play, for love and friendship.

There is no child alive who, at times, does not become angry at his parents, Dr. Baruch pointed out to his mother, Cathy. Hate exists side by side with love, ready to explode if love is weak or nonexistent. A child needs love to understand, accept, then control his rage. His basic hungers need to be nourished so his anger will not overwhelm him. If they are not, he will grow more demanding and, in one way or another, cling to immaturity as though it were his only salvation. Kenneth had not been allowed to show any sign of anger in his home.

Cathy started individual sessions with Dr. Baruch and during one she put her hands over her face, dug her nails into her cheeks and cried out, "I know it's all my fault! I'm no good for Kenneth. I should never have had a child. I really didn't want him." Her husband also did not want to be chained by a child, she said, but she had persuaded him after her mother had persuaded her.

She admitted she locked her son in his room at times because she felt she could not control her feelings and might hurt him as she once had tried to hurt her younger brother when they were children. In a rage, she had hurled him to the floor and banged his head against the floorboards, wanting to kill him. Then she stopped herself, stood up, pushed him into another room and locked the door to protect him from her fury.

Dr. Baruch realized that Cathy had been unable to nourish her son's "love-hunger" because of her own "love-hunger" as a child. Her parents had often made her feel like a nonentity; her father at times slapped her if she talked back.

Kenneth saw Dr. Baruch regularly for two and a half years, then occasionally for the next three years whenever he felt he wanted to go to her. She believed he could at last manage his feelings of rage without denying them. He had, she said, acquired a basis for "true *self-control*—for managing the outflow of feelings, neither denying them nor letting them run wild." He now understood what he could do and what he could not do in more realistic terms.

He realized that with her help he could feel certain pleasurable sensations in his body without believing they were "dirty" or "bad," as his mother had told him. He accepted that he had to control his sexual feelings not by blocking or denying or paralyzing them but by finding acceptable ways to express them in accordance with his age. He now found that playing baseball was one way of using up energy as was making strong friendships with both boys and girls.

He told Dr. Baruch frankly, "When I first started with you I didn't need time for playing. I didn't have one true friend then. Now I have lots. I think I need more time for myself and my friends."

Dr. Baruch concluded that "the realest part" of our childhood as we later picture it comes from what we recall as we remember what we saw and heard and felt around us and, even more, from what we have made of this in our mind. We received clues, either openly or subtly, as to what our parents thought of us and what they meant to each other. These clues are tied in to the thoughts and feelings within ourselves.

She said of a child: "His impressions spread their wings in fantasy and mate in flight with wishes that he often feels should-not-be and with guilt and anxiety. And these in turn let misshapen offspring wing their way into adulthood to destroy the richness of mating and loving and creation and birth."

In his book *Rebel without a Cause* Dr. Robert Lindner showed how direct the relationship may be between repressed emotions of fear, anger and guilt and a physical symptom. Lindner used the technique of hypnoanalysis to take a youth he called Harold back to childhood, then earliest infancy. Harold was able eventually to recall scenes he saw from his crib when he was between six and eight months old.

As a young man Harold had violently assaulted and tried to kill an older man whom he admitted reminded him strongly of his father. The man had called Harold obscene names, which had enraged him because they were related to some of his deepest, most dangerous wishes.

The book also dramatically revealed how traumatic it may be for a baby to witness parents in the act of sexual intercourse. At the time, the baby does not know what is happening but he will become frightened as he sees what he believes is his father striking his mother. The experience leaves a memory trace that may later affect his sexual and aggressive feelings drastically.

Harold was treated by Dr. Lindner when Harold became a "criminal psychopath" in a prison in an Eastern state for his attack on the older man. As a result of this study of Harold and other criminals, Dr. Lindner concluded that the psychopath was emotionally still a child bent on achieving instant gratification of his every wish, no matter how much it hurt him or others. Psychopathy, in essence, he said, was a prolongation of infantile patterns and habits into the stage of physiological adulthood.

Dr. Lindner further stated he believed the psychopath never progressed beyond the pregenital level of sexual development (concern only with the self) to the stage where he could love someone else (this was certainly true of Joel Steinberg). Hurtful experiences of early life became "fixated before the psychopath's adult, or genital level, was reached" (in Steinberg's case, this would explain the fury of his childhood wishes to hurt and kill both Hedda Nussbaum and little Lisa, originally directed at his parents, who, in vital ways, had to have crippled him emotionally). Lindner also noted the intense egoism of the psychopath, which he said was similar to a child's.

Harold was twenty-one when Lindner first saw him. His criminality began at twelve when, with other boys, he broke into a grocery store and robbed it of $75 worth of candy and tobacco. He engaged after that in a series of minor robberies, and was put on probation. When he was arrested for stabbing a man, this was a crime serious enough to warrant a heavy penalty.

He was Roman Catholic and spent the fourth to seventh grades in a parochial school after attending public school for the first three years. He left the parochial school to become a pupil in a special class for students with defective vision. At fifteen he graduated to high school, which he quit after a year. He gave up all attempts at study and worked sporadically on a relative's farm while looking in vain for a job. He always failed the eye tests.

His father, a machinist by trade, had come to the United States from Poland at the turn of the century. He married an American-born girl, they settled in an industrial suburb of a large Eastern city. Harold was their first child; two years later a daughter was born, then another daughter several years after that. The father fell ill with an occupational disease that forced him to give up his job in a factory. Investigators described him as a disciplinarian, more ready with curses and cruel words than blows, though Harold gave Dr. Lindner many examples of physical blows dealt him by his father over the years.

His mother, a worn and tired woman, according to the reports, described Harold's birth as normal and his childhood as healthy, except for an attack of measles at two, after which his eyes started to blink. She took him to doctors over the years, they found nothing physically wrong with his eyes and could not help him. He had 10 percent normal vision in the right eye, 15 percent in the left.

The many psychologists and psychiatrists who examined and tested Harold, while disagreeing as to what caused his life of crime, all agreed on a diagnosis of psychopathic personality, complicated by social difficulties stemming from the condition of his eyes. One psychiatrist reported he had "a subconscious jealousy of the father and a mother fixation." Harold had an IQ of 107.

Dr. Lindner's first impression of Harold was of a fairly tall, sparsely built boy with wide shoulders and narrow hips. His face was rather intelligent, the one feature that attracted immediate attention was his heavy-lidded, continually fluttering eyes that gave his face the almost masklike appearance of the totally blind, unless the observer noticed the restless, shifting play of the pupils and the fast blinking of the lids.

Harold at first seemed sneering and sullen, said he did not think treatment would help him but agreed to take part in the experiment with the new therapy. Dr. Lindner asked whether he would rather be blind than become able to keep his eyes open for longer periods. Harold replied, "I'd rather be blind than to see some of the things I have seen," but would not explain what he meant.

He entered the trance state rapidly and easily, obeying Dr. Lindner's instructions. In response to the suggestion his lids stay open and remain fixed and steady while a strong light was directed into his eyes, Harold opened his eyes and stared directly into the sharp light, something he never had been able to do. This convinced Dr. Lindner that Harold's condition, though essentially physical, had been caused by some traumatic psychological assault on him at a crucial stage in his very early development.

There were recorded in all, over a microphone concealed in the couch on which Harold lay, forty-six sessions. During the first few sessions, he discussed life at the prison and general topics such as current politics and marriage, saying he did not think he would ever marry.

During the third session, Harold mentioned his father. He said he hardly ever spoke to him because they never got along. He recalled that once, when he was thirteen, his mother told him to call his father, busy fixing tires in the garage, into the house for supper and his father picked up a hammer and threatened to hit him with it. He remembered when he was fifteen his father and mother had quarreled and his father struck his mother, knocked her to the floor. Harold picked up an iron poker and was about to hit his father with it but his sister pulled it out of his hands.

When he was a boy, he joined a gang that stole bicycles, cars, food, sometimes set fires in empty houses. Most of the boys had rifles and knives they had stolen. He fought with boys who taunted him because of his eyes. He told Dr. Lindner he thought people did not like him because his eyes kept blinking and when they made remarks about his eyes he felt like choking them or hitting their heads against the side of a building.

During the tenth session Harold informed Dr. Lindner that his eyes had improved, he could open them much wider and they did not blink as much, even in the sunlight. The following session Harold spoke of his longing for sex while in prison; he said he had occasionally experimented with girls in high school. He mentioned his closest friend in the jail, Perry, who tried constantly to seduce him into a homosexual affair. Harold would not give in, though he said he had considered it because he liked Perry and did not want to lose his friendship. He compared Perry to his mother in that they each had a pitiful, helpless look. He told Dr. Lindner he had once been sexually involved with a man.

Threaded throughout the remaining sessions were recollections of the many beatings his father gave him. He said his mother was usually kind to him though occasionally she beat him too. But she stood up for him when his father ridiculed him. She would give him money to go to the movies so he would be out of the way when his father came home from work.

At the next session he described the brutality of a priest in the parochial school who struck pupils so hard with his cane that one boy collapsed on the floor. Harold also confessed he stole guns because he liked the noise and the vibrations when the gun went off. A gun, he said, gave him a feeling of courage, imbued with the thought he was "a man."

He recalled, the following session, of seeing his mother partially nude in the bathtub in the middle of the kitchen, where everyone took baths. She always asked him to wash her back. He said he did not like doing this but whenever he objected she would "swing around and hit me."

He remembered seeing his sister naked when she took baths. He also recalled that when he was ten and his sister eight they took naps on summer afternoons, encouraged by their mother in what he called "a cradle . . . like a junior bed." At these times he would fondle his sister all over. He recalled having intercourse with her five or more times.

At the next session he again mentioned his dislike of his father, recalled as a boy hearing his parents at night in the next room preparing for intercourse. He hated to hear their voices and what they said, would cover his head with the blanket. During this session he also remembered his father once told him he was going to cut off his son's penis and give it to his sister, who was a tomboy. Another time his father threatened to sic the dog on him, saying she would bite off his penis. His mother overheard, and scolded his father for such a threat.

The thirty-fifth hour yielded a gold mine as far as memory was concerned. Harold spoke of his eyes improving, then under hypnosis recalled a time when, as a baby, he had slept in a cradle with squared wooden bars that stood between his parents' bed and a bureau. The cradle was placed to the right of the bed. Often in the morning, after his father left for work, his mother would take him into bed with her. He remembered that, as a matter of habit when he woke, he would look over to see if she was in bed or had gone to the kitchen.

Then, speaking with "much overt expression of pain and suffering," according to Dr. Lindner, Harold recalled an episode that related directly to his physical symptoms. He told again how he would wake up in the morning to see the sun shining into the room, then look over at his parents' bed to see if his mother was in it. If she was, he would make a noise so she would come over and pick him up.

But this one morning, a Sunday, when he woke, he looked at the bed and saw his parents having intercourse. His mother became aware he was staring at them, said something to his father and they got out of bed. He recalled seeing and being frightened of his father's genitalia because they were "big, so big." He compared them to "a vicious animal," as though his father had used them to attack his mother. He again mentioned the sun "shining, shining into the room," then spoke of his fear that his father had hurt his mother and would hurt him.

During the next session Harold, again in a deep hypnotic trance, confessed he had murdered a man (the man lived but Harold at first believed he had killed him). Harold described how an older man who had spent time in jail, with whom he occasionally played cards, and who cheated, had been playing pool at a table next to him one night.

Harold pulled his stick back to make a shot and accidentally struck this man on the elbow. The man cursed him, Harold apologized. The man called him "a lying mother-fucker," and other obscene names. Harold went home agitated, saying he had often slept with his mother in the same bed until he was fifteen when she had fights with his father, but "I would never even touch her." He remained in a daze for about a week. Then he decided to get even with this man. He caught up to him on the street one day, pulled out a hunting knife he had stolen a few years before from his father, and plunged the knife into the man's neck several times, then into his chest and finally "way down." He left the man lying on the street, believing him dead.

At this point Harold again recalled the morning he had seen his parents naked on the bed. He remembered how, after his mother had picked him up and placed him in the high chair in the kitchen, his father had looked "mad," his enraged black eyes "shining" as though he wanted to hit his son.

Dr. Lindner said it was evidently at this moment that Harold's eyes first started to become affected. He described sitting in the high chair, his father talking to him. Harold said haltingly, "I don't understand what he is saying. I'm afraid of him. . . . And his eyes, they look all lit up. . . . The light is coming right at me, two little darts. Before they were bright, now they are smaller. I can't see anything else. . . . Everything is black, blacker, I see nothing." He said his eyes hurt so acutely that he felt an ache in the back of his brain, as though someone had stuck a knife into his eyes.

Dr. Lindner asked why the lights were coming from his father's eyes. Harold said that when he lay in the cradle and saw his father on top of his mother, his mother looked at him and her eyes were soft and pitiful but his father's eyes were hard, "like bright lights." He added that he saw "the whites, looking right into my eyes, shining." Then he said, "I don't know whether I am afraid of his eyes or his penis more. They're mixed. His eyes—his penis."

While Harold was still in the deep trance, Dr. Lindner asked him to remember even further back and Harold recalled a time he was about six months old and drinking from a bottle. His father sat nearby, his eyes had "green in them but they were not shining." Only the sun was shining and his own eyes did not blink. The blinking started only after he saw his mother and father having intercourse. An intercourse he had once later interrupted, to the wrath of his father.

Then he spoke of his "accident," when he stabbed the man on the street. He compared the man to his father in that he too was strong, "tough," had a large chest. Harold said he thought maybe when he stabbed the man he was getting even with his father for all the times he had beaten him.

Dr. Lindner asked Harold the origin of his hate for his father and Harold replied, "I—I . . . you know. That—what—I—saw. . . . My mother and my father. . . . He was—hurting—her."

Dr. Lindner further pointed out that the man in the poolroom had accused Harold of being "a mother-fucker," of doing the same thing

Harold saw his father doing—having sexual intercourse with his mother. Dr. Lindner explained that the man, by Harold's own admission, had reminded him of his hated father who, also by his own admission, he had wanted to get rid of so he could have his mother all to himself.

At this moment Harold started to sob. For about ten minutes he was incoherent. Such reaction to a therapist's interpretation means the therapist has uncovered a deeply buried fantasy, in this case a fantasy related to both sexual intercourse and violence.

After he stopped crying Harold said he felt better. He said he really did not hate his father, he loved his mother—and that was one reason he did not carry out his plan to kill his father. He told Dr. Lindner this was the first time in a long while he felt relieved, his shoulders and arms seemed lighter.

The following session Dr. Lindner started to interpret to Harold what had really happened, as shown by his memories, dreams and thoughts. Dr. Lindner mentioned the many times Harold spoke of moving to get out of the way of the "lights" in his father's eyes after seeing his parents in bed and imagining his father was hurting his mother (the way most children interpret the act of intercourse).

When Harold first saw his father's enormous (to him) penis, the sight was difficult to bear, alien and dangerous. Because Harold thought he was seeing something forbidden, confirmed by the furtive actions of his parents upon being discovered in the act of sex, he felt extremely guilty, as though he witnessed something forbidden to him. He feared the wrath of his father because he, the son, was an interloper. The "light" in his father's eyes was a look of anger, one he sought to escape from then on, hence the blinking of his eyes to avoid light.

Because of this experience, Dr. Lindner pointed out, and because "of the intrinsic character of your father, because of the kind of person he was"—a man who threatened to cut off his son's penis, a father who constantly rejected and humiliated him—Harold grew up hating his father and hating himself. (Dr. Lindner did not mention his mother's seduction of him, to a certain extent, by insisting he wash her back while she lay naked in the bathtub. Or her encouragement of his incestuous behavior by allowing him to sleep in the same bed with his sister.)

Dr. Lindner told Harold he had carried with him over the years an overwhelming guilt at his wish to take his father's place with his mother, a natural wish in every son when he is about three or four as the oedipal conflict develops. Dr. Lindner also explained to Harold he had used a knife, rather than a gun, to attack the man who maligned him because the knife was, for Harold, a symbolic representation of the penis. He had once stolen a knife from his father as he might wish to steal his father's penis. He feared his father might take away his own penis, as he had actually threatened to do, because of his incestuous wishes for his mother. His few early, hurried sexual escapades were attempts to convince himself he was a man, that his father had not castrated him in retaliation for his wish to kill his father.

Harold had denied what he had seen as a baby, burying it in the unconscious part of his mind, believing it would thus disappear, as he built defenses against its emergence into his consciousness. He knew his thoughts were forbidden and felt frightened and guilty. But his fear, wish and guilt appeared in his loss of sight, as though he could not bear to look at the people in his crazy world.

During his forty-first hour Harold recalled another experience, one that fitted more of the pieces of his early life into place. He recalled what had happened the night before he saw his parents having intercourse. It was a Saturday night and his mother and father had taken him to a movie. He remembered men with big hats, cowboys with guns and a wolf or a dog. Harold said he half lay, half sat in his mother's arms.

He spoke of bright rays of light emanating from the projection room and flashing on the screen—two separate rays. He saw the heads of men and women in the audience around him. He reached up to touch his mother and she put his hand down, wanting to watch the movie. Turning his head over his mother's shoulder he saw again the rays of light. They seemed to shoot at him and he was frightened.

The next morning as he sat in the high chair, Harold recalled he saw once again the lights of the night before, this time as though glaring out of his father's eyes. He started to cry and his mother picked him up and rocked him in her arms.

Three sessions later Harold remarked that his eyes were a hundred percent better, that there was nothing really worrying him now, though he had the feeling "of a longing for loneliness." He knew the sessions were nearing their end and was trying to hide his disappointment, Dr. Lindner explained to him.

He asked Dr. Lindner to go over what had happened in the previous forty-five sessions. Dr. Lindner explained that many of his conflicts went back to that one traumatic morning and the night before when he was taken to the movies—both experiences new and frightening to a baby.

Harold had finally remembered his father's face, lit up in the dark theater, and scenes from the movie that frightened him when he saw the wolf or dog on the screen. The next morning, when he saw something he was dimly aware he should not see because his mother pushed his father away from her and pointed guiltily to Harold, his father seemed angry, as though he wanted to hurt him (and actually punished him often in later life). Dr. Lindner explained to Harold that to children so very young, all time becomes as one, with no sharp lines dividing day and night.

Harold had tried to escape his fear by closing his eyes, the guilty organs, for they had seen what was forbidden—the sight in the bed that had caused so much agony, jealousy and guilt.

Fear of his father and his father's large penis had followed him as he stole guns and knives, trying to prove himself as good a man as his father. His excessive masturbation was also a way of fighting his father, especially since his father had threatened to cut off his penis. Such a threat is a very frightening one to a child or young boy. Dr. Lindner also pointed out that Harold's parents had deep emotional problems that affected their children in many unhappy ways.

In summarizing the case, Dr. Lindner declared that it offered a striking illustration of the truth of a remark made by the psychiatrist Dr. William Alanson White—that behind every criminal deed lies a secret. Dr. Lindner added that what is more important, however, is that "we have glimpsed the utter futility, the sheer waste, of confining individuals in barred and turreted zoos for humans without attempting to recover such secrets." He called Harold's case "a mockery of current penological pretense."

He pointed out that Harold nearly killed a man in response "to those ungovernable needs which came flaring up from the deepest, remotest shafts of his being. Had he not undertaken analysis, all the trade-training, all the attentions of penal personnel would have been wasted on him. Had he not undertaken analysis . . . his conflicts would have been driven more deeply and his hostility aggravated by a system that flatters itself that it is doing other than substituting psychological for physical brutality."

Dr. Lindner reported that during the sessions Harold had gained insight and a real understanding of the past and how it had affected his attitudes and goals. He not only saw more clearly but felt better and behaved more like a twenty-one-year-old. Those who knew him commented on his change. Dr. Lindner concluded, "Gone is that sneering sullenness, that arrogant aggression, that Storm-Trooper mentality, that disregard for the rights and feelings of others. He knows that he was a psychopath: he knows why he was a psychopath: he knows that he needs to be a psychopath no more."

We have Dr. Lindner to thank for a moving account of how a physical handicap was caused by powerful emotional scenes that took place in the life of a very young child. The fears aroused at that time and the cruelties the father later inflicted on his son almost made the son blind, turned him into a semicriminal. Hopefully, his life was changed through the new awareness he received during the sessions with Dr. Lindner.

Another way our body is affected by our fantasies is through overeating and undereating (*anorexia nervosa*). Both extremes punish the body and are caused by childhood fantasies and rage at the mother that starts during the early feeding period. The anorexic, by sometimes literally starving herself to death, is holding back a murderous rage at a mother and/or father she believes does not love her.

Much physical illness could be avoided if people became more aware of the anger bubbling within that finds a partial outlet by menacing the body in some way as a signal that life is not felt as happy or peaceful.

10 Rage and Creativity

Many artists, actors, writers and other creative men and women have lived with a deep anger within since childhood, unaware of its destructive depths. They have managed successfully to direct some of the rage into rewarding work.

"Talent is so often the scar tissue over a wound," as Elia Kazan puts it in his book *The Life*.

Biographies of creative people who have undergone psychoanalysis (some of the books describe the analysis in part) attest to this as do the records of therapists who have treated creative, angry men, women and adolescents. As a result of facing the pain in their lives, they have become far more creative, needing less psychic energy to hold back their feelings of rage.

Two of the most creative men of the past endured childhoods that clearly show how their rage started. Biographies of Vincent van Gogh speak of the early death of his mother, the loving care his brother took of him, providing shelter and money as he painted glorious works of art that eventually sold for millions of dollars, breaking the records of all other paintings. Committed to a mental institution, feeling he would never be a success, he killed himself because of a deep depression before one of his paintings had been sold.

Van Gogh evidently never felt manly. Just before he committed suicide, he sliced off an ear and sent it to a prostitute. The mutilation of an ear, as Freud points out, stands for castration. Perhaps van Gogh had been impotent with the prostitute or perhaps he was sending her his penis symbolically, telling her that he was the woman, she, the man. Only he knew what his fantasies were. But his act told of a deep rage buried under the depression that closed in on him.

Then there is the rage within Franz Kafka, of which he wrote both directly, in the book *Letter to His Father,* and indirectly in all his novels, including *The Metamorphosis.* The latter was performed recently on Broadway with Baryshnikov playing the role of Kafka's fictional counterpart, Gregor Samsa. In the actual letter Kafka wrote to his father, asking his mother to relay it (she never did, perhaps believing it would hurt his father too deeply), he called his father an "authoritative man" who imposed "heavenly commandments" on his son, not permitting Kafka to "form a judgment of the world, above all, form a judgment of you, yourself."

He accused his father of making him a slave as he "lived under laws that had been invented only for me and which I could, I did not know why, never completely comply with." He spoke of himself as "continually in disgrace; either I obeyed your orders, and that was a disgrace, for they applied, after all, only to me; or I was defiant, and that was a disgrace too, for how could I presume to defy you; or I could not obey because I did not, for instance, have your strength, your appetite, your skill, although you expected it of me as a matter of course; this was the greatest disgrace of all."

Declaring that in his later life "I fled everything that even remotely reminded me of you," he described his efforts to be different as "slightly reminiscent of the worm that, when a foot treads on its tail end, breaks loose with its front part and drags itself aside." Here he visualized himself as a worm, later, a cockroach.

This brief book, holding only the contents of one letter never delivered, is a masterpiece not only in its style of writing but in the description of the anguish of a boy, then a young man, growing up under the power of a sadistic, cruel, unsympathetic father. But at least Kafka was able to transform some of his murderous wrath into literature that will live as long as man can read.

Those who write fictionally of murder and the anger within the murderer have found a way to express some of their early murderous feelings, one that brings fame and fortune. Thomas Harris in *The Silence of the Lambs* and *Red Dragon* writes of unbelievably vicious killers, tying their motives to cruelty in childhood at the hands of parents. We hear the voice of the child emotionally crucified by parents who hated, neglected or abandoned him.

A woman writer of successful mystery stories told a friend, "If I am not at my typewriter pouring out words that fill in the plots I have outlined, I feel unfulfilled. It's as though I only come alive, deserve to live, when I am writing. Cooking two meals a day for my husband is not enough for my ego."

The art of expressing her raging feelings through her fictional victims and their killers allows her to dilute temporarily the anger in her heart against those who hurt her in childhood, adolescence and possibly the present. She feels depressed if she does not have the outlet of writing of her rage.

Some writers, like the late Nelson Algren, who refused to enter analysis because he thought it would destroy his creative ability, run away from facing their rage. Algren no doubt could have enjoyed a happier life with his marital partners had he been free to acknowledge some of his unreal rage of childhood.

Creative people who have gone into psychoanalysis write of its benefits and how it helped them know what they really felt. This enabled them to become even more creative. Famous comedian Sid Caesar, author of a chapter, "What Psychoanalysis Did for Me," in *Celebrities on the Couch,* edited by this writer, said, "I was a success. I had a lovely and devoted wife, a darling little girl. The future looked bright. I was miserable."

He posed the question, "What did my analysis do for me in concrete terms?" And answered: "First, it made me aware of the eruptions and upheavals of anger and resentment, murderous drives developed in childhood, which had no outlet—the very feelings which could have turned me into a delinquent. In one sense, I was a delinquent; I had to take those feelings out on someone. I took them out on the nearest person to me—myself. I wouldn't let myself be happy for any money."

He said that once he made it clear to himself that those childhood incidents were in the past, he started a new life. One in which "I was no longer a child but a grown man, and because I was grown, no problem could loom as large as it had in the days when I was surrounded by giants."

His work started to improve, he was able to get done in a few hours what before took an entire day because he no longer wasted so much time "worrying over and cherishing my neuroses." He said it helped reach a deeper feeling "for the idiosyncrasies and foibles on which so much humor is predicated. It used to be that a good deal of my comedy made sport of people. In a sense, it was another outlet for my inner anger, for satire is angry humor. Now, I try to use myself as a mirror in which others can see their behavior."

He found he was less irritable at home, that he now regarded his wife, who also went into analysis, "not only as someone I'm married to, but as my dear friend, someone who understands me and someone on whom I can lean when I have to."

He summed it all up, he said, in the words, "I found that, by developing self-respect, you will inevitably learn to respect others."

In the same book Jayne Meadows, a Broadway actress, film star, television personality and wife of Steve Allen, wrote of her experience, titled "The Two Jaynes," which told how she went into psychoanalysis because she suffered a number of mysterious allergies. She had undertaken a failed marriage with a man more than twice her age and was not enjoying acting in Hollywood. She found a brilliant and sensitive psychiatrist "who gave me the courage and strength to break the unusually strong, neurotic ties with my family of childhood and see it was possible for me to really love my parents in a healthy way. For the first time I was able to see them as human beings with human weaknesses and not as the all-powerful authority figures which had so frightened me in the past."

She said psychoanalysis also made it possible for her "to believe in God with a conviction born of love, not fear. My favorite book, the Bible, asks us: What good is it if you win the world and lose your own soul? Well I say, what good is it if you win the whole world and lose your own child? For our children are what we make them."

Under the chapter title "The Reluctant Hero," James "Jim" Patrick Brosnan, a major league pitcher, turned writer, author of two nonfiction books about the world of baseball, *The Long Season* and *Pennant Race*, described how he happened to go into analysis.

He was playing in the Chicago Cubs minor league system, his first year in organized baseball, "what was to be the first of nine lonely years in the minor leagues." He was not doing well, wrote to a friend describing himself: "Shortness of temper; unwarranted dislike of people in general; loss of sense of humor, ambition, human understanding."

He found out later that the Cubs' general manager, Jim Gallagher, had gone to Arthur Meyerhoff, head of his own advertising agency and a stockholder in the Chicago Cubs, also known for his interest in psychoanalysis. Gallagher said to Meyerhoff, "We've got a boy who has great talent as a pitcher but he's also got problems. What do you suggest?"

"Bring him to me," said Meyerhoff.

At Gallagher's suggestion Jim went to Meyerhoff's office on Michigan Avenue in the famed Wrigley Building. Meyerhoff suggested he go into psychoanalysis for which the Cubs had offered to pay.

Jim said dubiously, "I'm not sure a psychoanalyst could do me any good."

"Why don't you try?" Meyerhoff suggested.

Jim said, "I'll think about it."

Meyerhoff gave Jim the name of Dr. George Mohr. Jim made an appointment to see Dr. Mohr and then started the process of understanding his inner self. After a few months he found he could discuss his life more freely, "especially my feelings about my father. He and I always had a strained relationship. I started to understand that this was the basis for my rebellion against managers, umpires or any sort of authority," including especially the umpires (his father had been an umpire for a while).

Jim also realized it was not just one parent who contributed to his lack of cooperation with authorities but also his mother—he felt both, in a sense, were his enemies. His mother, a former nurse, was a very intelligent woman who loved music and reading in contrast to her husband whose only interest was baseball. (In time Jim would combine their interests, becoming both a famous professional baseball player and a writer.)

Jim soon trusted Dr. Mohr enough so he could talk "about another subject that had been unconsciously troubling me—my sexuality. I had indulged in three brief romances, none lasting longer than a month. I had never thought of forming any enduring, intimate relationship with a woman. It was obvious to me that I was not the aggressor, even in my short romances."

One night at a party he met a very attractive young woman, Anne Stewart Pitcher, discovered they had at least two things in common— baseball and music. They were married on June 23, 1952, and had a baby three years later. Jim had a relaxed relationship with his wife and also began to make friends among his teammates.

When his work with Dr. Mohr ended, he started to keep a diary. Part of it was published in *Sports Illustrated*. This led to his first book, *The Long Season*, which sold well. He was now pitching for the Cincinnati Reds and played in the World Series, helping to win the pennant in 1961.

In spite of all this success, he again felt depressed and decided to go back into analysis. Dr. Mohr had left Chicago to practice in Los Angeles so Jim went to Dr. Lucia Tower whose offices were located in the Chicago Institute for Psychoanalysis on North Michigan Avenue. The help given by her and Dr. Mohr, he wrote, "allowed me to communicate first, with myself, second, with Anne, and finally, with other people."

He said he felt that without that help he did not think he could have played professional baseball, then conducted a successful television program about the sports scene in Chicago, or written two books about baseball and a novel: "In looking back, I feel that my analysis, my marriage and knowing Art Meyerhoff were the most important steps I took toward a fuller, more satisfying life. I have reached an understanding of myself and know now that people are good to know for what they are, and not for what I am to them or can get out of them."

No doubt his analytic treatment enabled the creativity in him to flow more freely so that he could write both fiction and nonfiction. As he could face, as he said, the rage of his childhood both at his mother and father, he understood himself far better. He also was able to make a good marriage in which both he and his wife realized neither was "perfect," could never be, but they loved each other anyhow.

Vivian Vance, first known to America's television viewers from *I Love Lucy* and *The Lucy Show*, under the chapter title "No More 'Shoulds,'" wrote that after her analysis she would "wake up every morning and face the day with joy . . . accept the day with its joys and sorrows, instead of feeling depressed and despairing."

She went on, "A new well of vitality has burst within me and has never run dry. Analysis gave me a great release of energy. Some people fear analysis because they feel it will diminish their talent. They believe their neurosis is making them talented. But analysis made me more aware of my resources. I don't care about the work so desperately. I work for joy, and for the money. And I used to work so hard to get everyone's approval. Now I only care about my own approval."

She described aptly why she had picked the "wrong mate" (which she said she found out, thanks to analysis). She said, "When you marry neurotically, your least desirable qualities emerge. All your hostile projections rise up to clash with those of your partner. The anger and feelings of ambivalence stem from childhood and relate to your attitudes toward your parents. You marry someone like your parents, wanting their approval just as you wanted the approval of your parents. You are constantly living for someone else's actions and reactions rather than living out your own life."

Richard Florsheim, internationally known painter and printmaker, represented in fifty museums throughout the world including the Metropolitan Museum of Art and the Museum of Modern Art in New York and the Art Institute of Chicago, his hometown, said that his psychoanalysis involved "every aspect of my life." This included feelings of guilt, fear and shame, which took a long time to face in treatment.

He admitted, "I went into analysis with a chip on my shoulder, afraid, as are many artists, that it would destroy my creative drive. I told the analyst this. She said, 'If you are really creative, you will emerge from treatment even more so. If you are not really creative, is it not better to find it out now, while you are young?'"

He recalled, "I dove into analysis with everything I had. For me, it was like reaching for a life preserver miraculously encountered in an endless ocean. It was a matter of life or death, of basic survival."

He remained only two years, felt analysis was not finished, and said, "I think analysis never really finishes neatly and cleanly. . . . There are many paradoxes and contradictions in life and in analysis, as part of life. If I find it necessary, I will go back into analysis."

He found, however, he could derive his satisfactions from his work, for it "began to flow, improve and change." He also learned "not to run away from myself." He married, had a summer home in Provincetown and made frequent trips to Europe.

He concluded, "Analysis helped me to realize how much of my energy was used up in fighting unresolved battles, in running around in a circle trying to catch my own tail. I do not think that it lessened my artistic productivity. It increased it and changed its focus. My creative drive was released, not destroyed."

Graham Greene, author of many novels including *The Heart of the Matter, The Third Man* and *The Quiet American,* said of his psychoanalysis in London, where he stayed with his analyst several months, "Those months were perhaps the happiest of my life."

Eddie Jaffe, a leading public relations specialist throughout the world, whose accounts have included the US Treasury Law Enforcement Agencies, the governments of Indonesia and Iceland and leading movie and stage stars, was in analysis six years with one of the country's leading psychoanalysts.

He summed up, "My analysis taught me that I didn't have to allow my childhood to have such an undue influence on my adult life. Also, it gave me the understanding that anger, impatience and rudeness displayed toward me by others is not my problem but that of the person indulging in such behavior."

He added, "To those who believe that drugs or other magic remedies can replace the long, expensive, painful road to self-knowledge, I can only ask, 'Will the pill help us to love?'" He described the analyst's main role as "preventing the patient from continuing the self-delusions that serve to protect all of us from facing the truth about ourselves." He added, "I was kept from continuing my self-deception, hiding behind defenses that had made my life painful and frustrating, not realizing that facing them would prevent the pain and frustration."

Floyd Patterson, former heavyweight champion of the world at twenty-one and the only boxer in his class to have regained the title after losing it, wrote an autobiography, *Victory over Myself,* with Milton Gross, the writer. He was interviewed for his story in *Celebrities on the Couch* at his fight camp in Marlboro, New York, where he was in train-ing for the bout against Cassius Clay, to take place on November 22, 1965, in Las Vegas. He was trying to recapture his crown for a second time.

He told how at the age of eight he had started stealing dresses for his mother, who would never buy herself a new dress. They lived in the Bedford-Stuyvesant section of Brooklyn where he grew up, in one cold-water flat after another, always in need of more space as further babies arrived. Eventually there were eleven. His father, a longshoreman, worked hard to support his large family; his mother worked too, when she could as a maid or in a factory or caring for other people's children.

Patterson continued stealing, coming home with milk for the family. One day he was caught stealing a case of soda. A policeman chased him, and he was taken to court. A judge suggested he be sent to the Wiltwyck School for Boys in Esopus, New York, across the Hudson River from Poughkeepsie. There a teacher, Miss Vivian Costen, helped him feel he was not "stupid," bought him candy, told him it was all right to be wrong at times, no one was perfect. She spent time with him, talking about the subjects he studied, helping him understand them. She invited him to her house nearby, gave him confidence in himself, made him feel he was important.

He said, "She was so kind and considerate and understanding that I wanted more than anything else in the world to please her. The only way I knew—or was able to—was to be what she wanted me to be."

It was at Wiltwyck he first put on boxing gloves and won the first three bouts of his life. He started to feel some self-esteem, no longer the angry little boy who defied the law. He recalled, "What I found at Wiltwyck was a sense of belonging. It helped me feel the equal of the next guy." He discovered the nightmares he had suffered all his life ended at Wiltwyck.

Wiltwyck taught him, among other things, to want to win. As he put it, "I fight for acceptance and recognition, so I can walk with any-one. I enjoy being a winner. The day I stop being pleased, I'll know something is wrong."

Patterson said he found it hard to hate, that he could never hate an opponent in the ring. His two older brothers were fighters but not as

successful as he. He was able to buy a comfortable home for his mother
in Mount Vernon. He is still grateful for what Wiltwyck did for him.
You cannot call it psychoanalysis but Ms. Costen and others gave him
a sense of self-esteem, made him feel less angry, less sorry for himself,
showed him a respect he never knew, were patient with him. They gave
him, he said, "a sense of the discipline that every fighter needs."

He summed up, "At a time in my life when I could have gone one
way or another, the right way or the wrong way, Wiltwyck headed me
in the right direction."

One of America's leading playwrights, William Inge, known for *Picnic, Bus Stop, The Dark at the Top of the Stairs,* and *Come Back Little
Sheba,* all of which were made into outstanding motion pictures, said
that psychoanalysis to him "seems to be the great learning experience
that the Twentieth Century can provide. Once one has worked through
this experience, he cannot help but have a more basic understanding
of human life and of all western culture."

While he did not think it a necessary experience for all writers, and
probably "it is not a meaningful experience to anyone who does not seriously need it," he said, "I believe that all writers who have undergone
analysis have been grateful for its broadening influence upon their insight."

Anyone who has been analyzed "can distinguish between those people prominent in our society and culture who have had experience 'on
the couch' from those who have not, and the former do appear to us
more humane, more deeply aware of human needs and more able to
face the complexity of life today," he concluded.

The late Hermann Hesse, winner of the Nobel Prize for literature,
who died in 1962, wrote an essay in 1918 in which he discussed the
effect of psychoanalysis on the creative spirit. Translated from the original German by Miriam M. Reik, it appeared in the *Psychoanalytic Review,* Volume 50, No. 3 in the fall of 1963.

Hesse declared that "the path of the psychoanalyst can, in fact, also
be of advantage to the artist. However wrong he would be to take analytic technique over into the artistic sphere, yet he would be right to
regard psychoanalysis seriously and to follow it."

He pointed out, "He who has earnestly gone some distance on the
path of analysis through memory, dreams and associations in search of
the primary spiritual sources retains as an enduring benefit what could
perhaps be called 'more intimate terms with his own unconscious.' He

experiences a warmer, more fruitful, more passionate back-and-forth between the conscious and unconscious; he takes what otherwise remains 'under the threshold' and what is only enacted in unnoticed dreams, and transfers much of it with him into the light."

He said of analysis that it "demands a sincerity towards oneself to which we are not accustomed. It teaches us to see, to acknowledge, to explore, and to take seriously exactly that which we have most successfully repressed. . . . Going back to mother and father, peasant and nomad, ape and fish, nowhere is the origin, relatedness and hope of man so earnestly and shakingly experienced as in a serious analysis. What you have learned will become visible, what you have known will become heartbeats, and when the anxieties, embarrassments and repressions are lifted, the significances of life and of personality is the more imperative matter.

"Neither the repression of the material which emerges from the unconscious, of uncontrolled ideas, dreams, playful phantasy, nor continued surrender to the shapeless eternity of the unconscious, but the loving listening to the hidden springs," permits "criticism and selection from the chaos—this is the way every great artist has worked," he stated. Added, "If any technique can help fulfill this demand, then it is psychoanalysis."

Hesse claimed that among the poets of the past who came very close to understanding the essential tenets of "analytic depth psychology" was Dostoyevski, who not only "intuited those roads which Freud and his students would travel long before they did," but also "possessed a true practice and technique of this kind of psychology."

It is not rage alone that makes for creativity, though it may act as a spur. Nothing is caused by any *one* thing, when it comes to the workings of the human mind. Many causes are contributors.

Psychoanalysts have discovered that often the creative process in childhood emerges because of the love of a mother or father who cherished the child, encouraged him to explore the beauty of the world outside his home—the colors of nature, of sunsets and clouds, flowers and pools of water, as Monet did.

Some believe the erotic feelings of the child were overstimulated by parents and this overstimulation was channeled into early creative endeavors. We might suspect this in the case of Georgia O'Keefe, some of whose paintings are extremely sensuous.

The creative spirit often comes to the rescue of someone whose life has been very unhappy. We might think perhaps of Beethoven, who never married, who claimed to have been miserable as he grew up but who produced music the world will never forget. The sublimation of rage in the long run fails to ease the psychic pain of the creator, but adds a certain satisfaction to his life that increases his self-esteem, at least for the moment.

11 When Self-Esteem Replaces Rage

Avaluable bit of advice was given by Confucius when he pointed out that a journey of a thousand miles begins with but "a single step."

In understanding the rage within us, the first step of admitting you feel anger starts you on the way to a deeper realization as to *why* you feel angry. This enables you then to allow yourself to *express* the emotion of anger, recall specific times in the past when you simmered with rage but dared not feel it.

If we are able to face the hidden feelings of our rage and know the wishes, fears and fantasies that once accompanied it, we lose the need to repress the anger that has been slowly eating at our mind. We become aware that some of our rage is justified and some is the result of intense fantasies and expectations that are unreal.

As we can admit the rage and its origins, we then feel more at peace with the world. We are in greater possession of what therapists call our "true self" as contrasted to the "false self." We no longer need the defense of denial based on illusions and hopeless wishes.

This means facing the helpless child still chained within. The child who could not express rage at his parents for fear he would lose their love and approval, perhaps be thrown out of the house or allowed to die from starvation. The vulnerability of a child is vast. He fears for his life if there is no one to take care of him.

We all have to make peace with our parents as, becoming adult, we realize no parent is "perfect," that a parent's life, too, holds fear and anger. We do this as we make peace with ourselves.

At times it is difficult reaching our fantasies. We may define "fantasy" as a mental activity usually expressing itself "in the form of ideas, events and images," as Kerstin Kupfermann, psychoanalyst, explains. She says, "Fantasy serves to express unconscious conflicts or to gratify unconscious and conscious wishes as well as being a preparation for realistic action appropriate to the requirements of the milieu."

Constantly during our life, she adds, "We are affected by the influence of unconscious and conscious fantasies in our awake life as well as when asleep. Freud said in 1911 that 'with the introduction of the reality principle, one species of thought activity was split off; it was kept free from reality testing and remained subordinated to the pleasure principle alone.' This activity is fantasying, which starts early in the play of children and later continues as daydreaming, abandons dependence on real objects."

Daydreaming is a universal activity, fantasies are the instruments for the expression of our instinctual drives, she points out, saying, "There are common clusters of fantasies which are concerned with important developmental issues from childhood, referred to, for instance, as the oedipal fantasy and the family romance fantasy."

Fantasy starts very early in life. The famous British psychoanalyst, Melanie Klein, believed the ability to fantasize begins in infancy long before verbal skills are acquired as the infant feels both aggressive impulses and destructive fantasies.

It is also important to know, as we look deeper into the self and come to terms with our anger, that, as Dr. Jacob Arlow describes it, "The nature of a person's fantasy life is peculiar to that individual. It is idiosyncratic, representing the specific compromise formations effected in response to conflicts growing out of childhood experiences, that is, out of the nature of the object relations, the traumatic events, unfulfilled wishes.

"These decisive forces of the individual's life are organized into a number of leading unconscious fantasies that persist throughout life. They form a stream of organized mental representations and wishes that act as a constant source of inner stimulation to the mind. Furthermore they create a mental set against which the data of perception are perceived, interpreted and responded to. The influence that they exert on the mind varies."

As Ms. Kupfermann points out, there is no exact information through research about how much time people spend fantasizing. But at the University of Chicago, studies by Michael Csikzentmihalyi have shown that our thoughts leave our actual tasks at hand from 10 to 20 percent of the day and a small fraction of that time is spent in fantasy. Most daydreams are transient. It is in our night dreams that our deepest fantasies appear and from them we may learn much about ourselves if, upon waking, we let our thoughts expand on the events of the dream.

To give an example, a forty-eight-year-old woman awoke from a dream in which she was in a strange house with her younger sister and suddenly turned to her, asked forlornly, "Tell me something. Was our father ever happy living here?" The father, an overworked producer of television shows, had just died of a heart attack.

The sister, in the dream, just stared at her, then said, "I don't know, I really don't know."

The woman, on waking, then remembered she had once asked her father, who left home when she was ten to marry a woman far younger than his first wife, the same question. She recalled hoping he would answer, "No, I was miserable in my second marriage. I wished I had stayed with all of you." Instead, he had looked at her thoughtfully, then said, "I've been very happy in this second marriage."

The dream showed her fantasy-wish that he *had* been miserable when he left his first family. It was not in accordance with reality but the dream gave outlet to her fervent desire, buried since she was a child, that her father would suffer for forsaking his wife and two daughters. Outlet, too, to her rage over the years at him for leaving *her* for another woman. At the age of ten, a little girl has strong fantasies of marrying her father.

As Ms. Kupfermann also points out, the ability to engage in vivid fantasizing is a way "of obtaining greater pleasure in everyday life; to make the boredom of it more acceptable; to cope with its daily stresses, its past and present traumas; to deal with emotions like anger; to enhance experiences such as the sexual ones. The content of these fantasies are mostly kept secret."

Some have to seek the help of a psychoanalyst if they are unable to face a painful past on their own. A twenty-nine-year-old woman, a literary agent, whose three-year marriage was collapsing, tried to hold her husband by stifling all her anger at him for having an affair with a secretary at his law firm.

A friend said to her one day, 'You can't swallow your rage and your pride, too. Go see a therapist and talk it out."

Reluctant at first, the woman decided she needed aid and sought a psychoanalyst who helped her understand that she had chosen as husband a sadistic, uncaring man, much like her father.

At first she protested to the analyst, "He doesn't look like my father in any way. The resemblance just isn't there."

"Ah, but does he *act* like your father?" the psychoanalyst asked.

She thought a moment, then said, "Come to think of it, he does. He's very authoritarian. And once he slapped me when I disagreed with him, which is what my father used to do."

"You sought the familiar," the psychoanalyst said. "Most women do.

If the familiar holds loving, benign feelings, the woman will be happy. But if the familiar resembles a tormented past, the woman will be unhappy."

Slowly the woman started to understand she wanted unconsciously to repeat the past relationship with her adored father. She had selected a man who treated her emotionally as her father did. One thing, psychoanalysts tell us, not recognized as a rule, is that when the father-daughter relationship has been too close, the taboo against sexual intimacy eventually operates in the marriage as it did in the woman's earlier life as a little girl in the thrall of the oedipal love.

It is important that men too not only understand their own conflicts but also understand those of the women. As well as the reverse—the women need to understand not only themselves but the emotions in the early life of the men. Each gender faces different problems.

One of today's greatest struggles between men and women occurs as women fight for their place in the working world, for the right to abortion and to have both home and career. Many men still want the woman to be docile, the caretaker at home, with no aspirations of her own.

Men do not understand woman's desire for equality—to be considered neither inferior nor superior but allowed a freedom long denied. As one woman said to another in the film *Steaming*, "Why don't men think we are as important as they are? Not better or worse. But as important."

A few famous masculine writers over the centuries dared describe women as superior to men. As America started to expand, following the country's successful revolt from the mother country England, the writer Alexis de Tocqueville, following a visit to the new nation wrote in his famous *Democracy in America* this tribute to women:

"If I were asked . . . to what the singular prosperity and growing strength of that people [Americans] ought mainly to be attributed, I should reply: To the superiority of their women."

In the mid-1880s Matthew Arnold, a British author, wrote of women: "If ever the world sees a time when women shall come together purely and simply for the benefit and good of mankind, it will be a power such as the world has never known." This sentiment is held today by some statesmen as well as by women's groups working for peace.

Henry Adams, American author, in 1907 wrote in *The Education of Henry Adams*: "Adams owed more to the American woman than to all the American men he ever heard of, and felt not the smallest call to defend his sex who seemed able to take care of themselves; but from the point of view of sex he felt much curiosity to know how far the woman was right, and, in pursuing this inquiry, he caught the trick of affirming that the woman was the superior. Apart from truth, he owed her at least that compliment."

Half a century later, in 1953, Ashley Montagu, in *The Natural Superiority of Women*, pointed out that everything men have said about almost any alleged "inferior race" they have said about women: their brains are smaller, their intelligence lower, they cannot be trusted to govern their own affairs, they are like children—emotional, uncreative, unintellectual.

There has been a "prejudice" against women, Montagu alleged, just as there has been a prejudice against racial and religious groups: "Man is himself a problem in search of a solution, and his prejudices against minority groups—and women constitute a social minority group if not a numerical one—are groping expressions of his confused attempts to solve his problem."

He suggests: "When men understand that the best way to solve their own problem is to help women solve those that men have created for women, they will have taken one of the first significant steps toward its solution. And what is woman's greatest problem? Man. For man has created and maintained her principal difficulties."

He also pointed out, illustrating the prevailing traditional attitudes toward women, that the entire article on women in the first edition of the *Encyclopedia Britannica*, published in 1771, consisted of the six words, "The Female of man. See *Homo.*"

Because of such derogation by men, women are still far from experiencing their aggressive wishes and acts as a sign of worth. Many have difficulty accepting the right to feel justified rage when humiliated or threatened in any way by a man or woman. Not enough women as yet feel they have the right to act like the wife in Ibsen's *A Doll's House.* She finally walked out on a husband who forbade her to undertake a career, wanted her only to serve him.

For centuries, before women constituted more than half the working force in this country, they depended on men for food, shelter, clothing. They dared not antagonize the source of their physical sustenance as they repressed all angry feelings. To them, any display of aggression meant loss of love from "the" man on whom they were dependent. They did not realize such love was based on their servitude, not on the expression of their capabilities and creativeness.

Many women today still believe they lack the right to assert themselves on the job. They find it difficult to speak up when they feel exploited in the workplace or demeaned by parent, employer, friend or colleague, not to mention husband or child.

A number of women have difficulty accepting their own capacities. One woman, who worked fifteen years for an international business corporation, confided to her husband, a lawyer, "I think my boss makes wrong decisions that cost the organization a lot of money. But I can't tell him that and risk losing my job."

A young wife remarked to her mother, "Even if I know my husband's wrong, why should I criticize him and make him angry? It's easier to swallow my pride, agree with his decisions and avoid a fight." She could, however, in a quiet way, if she disagreed with one of his decisions, have stated her point of view so she did not have to "swallow" her pride, then inwardly resent and hate him.

The relationship of repressed anger to self-esteem is a very close one. When we feel angry and repress the feeling, rather than admit and accept it, knowing we may or may not choose to act on it, we feel guilty. Guilt always lowers self-esteem, makes us feel worthless. Most of us are brought up with overstrict consciences and when we add prohibitions against the awareness, much less the display of anger, it is no wonder we find ourselves battling for self-esteem.

As Harriet Goldhor Lerner, a psychologist referred to earlier, says, "Feelings of depression, low self-esteem, self-betrayal and even self-hatred are inevitable when we fight but continue to submit to unfair circumstances, when we complain but live in a way that betrays our hopes, values and potentials."

Many of us do not manage our rage effectively, in a way that leads to awareness of the inner self. Instead, our way of trying to cope with anger is to hide it in the far reaches of the mind, believing it thus disappears forever. We are not aware it will "out" in ways that may haunt and harm us, emotionally and bodily.

We would feel far freer if, as Ms. Lerner puts it, "we can learn how to use our anger as a starting point to *change patterns* rather than *blame people.*"

This is true for men, too. One husband, an advertising executive, suffered for years with a wife who constantly accused him of "ruining" her life. He told a friend, "Mary says if she hadn't married me, she would have had a glorious career as an actress in the films. She blames me for everything that goes wrong in her life. From our son's failing a course in school to the cook's serving steak too well done for her taste."

"Why do you stay with her?" asked the friend.

"Because I don't have the courage to leave," he replied ruefully. "I always thought marriage was for life."

He finally decided to consult a therapist who helped him gain more self-esteem. He was able to talk frankly to his wife, who, in turn, went to a psychoanalyst. After receiving help and facing the conflicts within themselves, both were able to understand each other and save the marriage.

But many hide their anger and resentment over the years, then suddenly feel the guilt that accompanies buried rage and accept failure rather than success as marital partners, in careers and creative work. According to Roy Schafer, well-known psychoanalyst, in his article, "The Pursuit of Failure and the Idealization of Unhappiness," this is attributed to "unrealistic" guilt.

He points out that many men and women feel "the self must always fall short." They possess a severe conscience "with respect to which every pleasure must be paid for with painful guilt and self-destructiveness."

He believes the idealization of unhappiness is more conspicuous in women and the pursuit of failure more conspicuous in men. He cites the widespread victimization of women in our society and the discrimination against and brutalization of women (the battered wives), "not to speak of the many subtle forms of seduction of women into debased roles." All of these existing beliefs and acts play a large part in women taking in, developing and "rigidifying the unhappiness they subsequently have come to idealize," he says.

He gives as example a woman who tried to relieve others of their unhappiness "by absorbing it." He explained that unconsciously, as many women in our culture seem to do, "she incorporated their unhappiness and she suffered for others. In so doing, she felt she was being a 'good girl,' that is, kind, compassionate, supportive, undemanding, even self-sacrificing." From a young age, she had been doing this to an extreme degree with her mother, father, brother and two sisters.

As a result of psychologically taking in the unhappiness of her family, she "could more easily idealize them as kind, compassionate and supportive to her as a girl, and later as a woman," Schafer pointed out. In a sense she gained love and a certain stature in their lives by continuing to remain unhappy. But she added a false "sense of worth" to herself, feeling essentially a failure and was furious within because she so demeaned her capabilities.

Schafer quotes Freud's phrase, "those wrecked by success." A number of women (and men) fear success so intensely they bury all wishes to succeed. They do not dare accept even the smallest achievement on their part, try to hide any show of what they believe the aggressive spirit.

Schafer concludes that both success and failure stem from stresses and strains that hold "a devastating force because they are feared in terms of childhood experiences in attachment to parents, losses, defeats and other dangers."

Many men and women feel anxiety and guilt about their ambitious strivings or any show of competence. They apologize for the smallest success, feel depressed after the first moments of elation vanish. Thus they never achieve their highest potential in their chosen work, never find full satisfaction in whatever they do or enjoy moderate acclaim—because of guilt over possible success. Why does the thought of success cause such fear and guilt?

In their unconscious, "success" is equated with "murdering" those with whom they compete, someone to whom they are close. Success implies the vanquishing of a foe from the past—mother, father, brother, sister—someone who has caused ambivalent feelings in childhood. Someone who, at times, aroused rage and the wish for revenge.

It is not the *act* of surpassing parents or siblings in fame and fortune that causes guilt but the *fantasy* that such an act destroys the parents or siblings. To accept success without guilt is to achieve without the fantasy of revenge, which always carries with it the wish to kill. If you feel others will suffer because you achieve, you are suffering unwarranted guilt, demeaning yourself, denying yourself success.

We need to realize that success does not mean we wish to destroy those we envy or formerly envied as a child. Success is to be enjoyed, not denigrated or denied. Success can add immeasurably to a sense of self-esteem if guilt is absent. Or, if present, its causes are examined and accepted as unreal. No one drops dead at the thought of another's success.

As we can become aware of the difference between childhood wishes to destroy and realistic wishes to achieve—between hostile aggression at an early age and assertiveness as an adult—we free ourselves of the guilt of the past. If we make the distinction between our realistic right to achieve and our unrealistic fantasy of destroying those who once hurt us, we are able to seek success more freely, attain it and feel our rage slowly diminish.

Many of our conflicts may be understood as attempts to defend ourselves against, deny or hide our earlier rage perceived as dangerous to us. We have believed that in some way it would lead to the loss of the love of our mother and father when we were children. They became furious at us at times (unfairly, we always believed) but we had to hold our tongues and restrain our wish to lash out at them physically and with words.

Today more of us are accepting the idea that we need not feel the lowering of self-esteem as a hateful wish, knowing the wish is not the deed, as a child believes. The mature person realizes there is a world of difference between the wish and the act. He need not feel "bad" at the mere wish, no matter how murderous it may be.

For the greater emotional damage ensues if he dares *not* admit and then accept the rage he feels at demeaning himself or being demeaned by others, exploited in some hidden way. He now knows this rage, repressed instead of acknowledged, harms him far more than any unfaced wish.

As Shakespeare so wisely said in *Hamlet,* "Thus conscience doth make cowards of us all." Our conscience is often cruel to us, it may make judgments that are not realistic as the hidden fear inside us exerts its power over our conscience.

It is important for us to know when we possess the right to state firmly why we feel we are being exploited, maligned or treated unfairly, either by man, woman or child. A woman divorced twice from two angry men, the first an alcoholic who physically assaulted her, the second, an over-controlling, self-centered man, went to a psychoanalyst. Slowly she was helped to realize the anger she had concealed as she identified with the man. He acted it out for her (with herself as target so she could be punished for her "wicked" feelings).

After facing and accepting the rage that had been buried, she was able to find a more loving, understanding man. One who was not alcoholic or wished to dominate her but seemed interested in her as a human being with faults as well as virtues.

She told her mother, "I finally found a man who can be a friend as well as lover. He may not be as exciting to live with as the two emotionally disturbed men I married. But I feel more myself with him, far more at ease. And I respect him for respecting me, as well as for his thought-fulness."

This man accepted her as she was, which her mother and father had never done. Her father had attacked her in childhood and adolescence with words when she did not live up to his orders and expectations. He even slapped her occasionally for talking back as she fled in tears to her bedroom, wondered what she had done to offend him. As an only child, she bore all the complaints of her parents.

She had sought the same kind of angry, controlling man in her hus-bands until she finally realized she unconsciously wanted a man just like her father. A man who would perpetuate the unhappy, familiar past. As she became aware of this, she was free to love a man who was a "friend." Who did not need to strike her out of anger or boss her out of his need to control, or to possess the exalted "power."

She felt a new sense of strength within that came from allowing her-self to know the pain of a crippling past so she would no longer be driven to seek its repetition in adult life.

Some psychoanalysts believe it is easier for women than for men to examine the inner self when there is a failed marriage and thus gain a sense of self-esteem. As a woman feels greater respect for herself, she can more easily solve the problems that face her, including being head of a single-parent family, which is very important today. But more men are now accepting the need to understand the rage they have buried from childhood and are seeking therapy to alleviate their inner pain.

As stated earlier, it is very important to know the difference between aggression and assertiveness. As more men and women accept their right to assertiveness and to a hostile aggression when appropriate—reaction to bodily attack or psychological injury—they will be able to use what Dr. Henri Parens has called "nondestructive aggression." He explains that its aim is "to assert yourself upon, control, assimilate and thrust toward mastery of the self and the environment."

He describes nondestructive aggression as "a motivating force inher-ent in strivings for autonomy, nonhostile competitiveness and the se-curing and protection of one's needs, property and origin. It fuels assertiveness and self-determination, is intimately tied up with narcis-sistic aims and adaptation."

He points out that "to want to win a tennis match may be symbolic of wanting to destroy one's oedipal rival, but it may also represent the gratification of aggressive strivings that are neither hostile nor destructive and are closer to narcissistic (libidinal) strivings and mastery (ego function)."

The road to understanding the rage buried in the inner self is never a smooth one. The defenses against showing our rage openly are very strong—as strong as the child's wish to be loved and taken care of.

But the reward is very high. If we are able to face the past fears and furies, we reap high dividends of pleasure in our life. No longer do we need to keep fleeing vengeful feelings and fantasies that long ago were needed as protection against our rage bursting forth and costing us the love of parents.

We know now when our rage is warranted or when it emanates from unhappy moments of earlier days. Our "conscience" no longer makes us a "coward." We are afraid of no man. Where once there was unrealistic rage, there is now the feeling of courage. A courage that enables us to know parts of the inner self we formerly thought destructive and the willingness to speak up when we feel others are trying to destroy or manipulate us.

This is true courage. Battling not with the sword or the nasty word but with the quiet conviction that by becoming aware of the unreal rage of the past we may use our right to defend ourselves against the selfish and unrealistic behavior of others.

It is not easy to realize that in essence we stand alone. As Joseph Conrad said, "We are always alone, in our dreams and in life." But the more we become aware of the difference between real and unreal rage, the less we are alone in that our relationships with those we love become far more realistic and peaceful.

Where once anger raged, now understanding of the self leads to inner esteem. A sense of maturity pervades us as we no longer have to wage war with the demons within. The demons we once thought protected us but which we no longer need.

They were demons of our own making at a time we felt very vulnerable. Now we can give up unneeded fantasies, fueled by the past, and live in the world of reality. It is a quieter, less dramatic world but one that yields true inner peace.